The Positiv...

"F...ng rejected? Simon's book will change your mood in a
r......e! A marvellous book, positive, practical and inspiring...
...y freelance writer should keep a copy on their desk. If you're
...y to give up, just reach for this book – it re-ignites your
...g energy, effortlessly. It worked for me, and will work for

Cambridge – *Writers' News magazine's Agony Aunt*

...lliantly positive book by a brilliantly positive writer."
Galton – Prolific short story writer and author of *Passing
...ws, Helter Skelter* and *The Dog With Nine Lives.*

...ng is, in many ways, like any other job. You need talent
...nacity to succeed – but from time to time, you also need a
...ncouragement to stay positive. *The Positively Productive*
...offers practical advice to help you harness your confi-
...and keep your writing goals in sight."
Ashdown – Award-winning author of *Glasshopper* and
...*Up and Wait.*

...uinely helpful in encouraging new writers to manage their
...well, and to believe in themselves."
Long – Bestselling author of *The Bad Mother's Handbook* and
...*owing Grandma* and *Mothers and Daughters.*

"Simon Whaley's advice for writers is sensible, practical and inspiring. The Positively Productive Writer delivers a well-judged kick up the butt for writers everywhere."

Jane Wenham-Jones – *Writing Magazine columnist, novelist, and author of 'Wannabe A Writer?' and 'Wannabe A Writer We've Heard Of?'*

"After reading Simon's book I thought I might feel a bit more positive as an author. What I actually felt was an overwhelming motivation to sit at my laptop and write, write, write! He's totally changed my thoughts on rejection and I love the section on daily brainwashing. I don't think I'll ever get in my own way again!"

Heather Bestel – www.alittlebitofmetime.com

Simon Whaley's latest book, THE POSITIVELY PRODUCTIVE WRITER, will delight any rejection-weary scribe. It encapsulates all there is to say about how you can improve your writing skills in a very positive manner. We've long been asserting that positive thought works. Simon explains exactly how to use it to achieve your writing dreams. Buy this book. We wish we'd written it!

Cass and Janie Jackson – www.flair4words.co.uk

The Positively Productive Writer

How to Reject Rejection and
Enjoy Positive Steps
to Publication

The Positively Productive Writer

How to Reject Rejection and
Enjoy Positive Steps
to Publication

Simon Whaley

COMPASS
BOOKS

Winchester, UK
Washington, USA

First published by Compass Books, 2012
Compass Books is an imprint of John Hunt Publishing Ltd., Laurel House, Station Approach,
Alresford, Hants, SO24 9JH, UK
office1@o-books.net
www.o-books.com

For distributor details and how to order please visit the 'Ordering' section on our website.

Text copyright: Simon Whaley 2010

ISBN: 978 1 84694 851 0

A CIP catalogue record for this book is available from the British Library.

Design: Stuart Davies

Printed in the UK by CPI Antony Rowe
Printed in the USA by Offset Paperback Mfrs, Inc

We operate a distinctive and ethical publishing philosophy in all
areas of our business, from our global network of authors to
production and worldwide distribution.

CONTENTS

Acknowledgements   xii

Introduction – New Start, New You, New Writer   1

Part I – Setting Achievable Writing Goals   5

Goals   6

Reviewing Goals   17

Rewards   23

A Writing Buddy   26

Part II – Learn To Look On The Bright Side Of Life   29

Twisting Negatives Into Positives   30

The Truth Behind Rejection   33

Reviewing Your Work   41

Start Your Next Project Immediately   47

Booster Cards   49

Achievement Files   56

Brainwashing   61

Luck   64

Motivation   67

Part III – Putting It Into Practise   71

Finding The Time To Write   72

Brain Training   83

Writer's Block Doesn't Exist   87

The Write Place   93

Notebooks   96

Generating Ideas   98

Ten (foot) Steps To Productive Writing   105

Doing A Fagin   109

Lists   115

Quick Wins   125
Networking   132
Workshops / Seminars / Holidays   141
Confidence   150
Literary Festivals   154
Writing Magazines   157

Part IV – A Positive Writer's Year – Strategies To Succeed 159
A Positive Writer's Year   160
A Positive Farewell   181
Index   184

Other books by Simon Whaley:
100 Ways For A Dog To Train Its Human
100 Muddy Paws For Thought
Puppytalk – 50 Ways To Make Friends With Your Puppy
Running A Writers' Circle
Best Walks in the Welsh Borders
Fundraising For A Community Project
The Little Book of Alternative Garden Wisdom
The Bluffer's Guide to Banking (by Robert Cooper and Simon Whaley)
The Bluffer's Guide to Hiking

Contributed To:
The Freelance Photographer's Project Book
100 Greatest Walks in Britain
100 Stories For Queensland

This book is dedicated to *all* writers who sit down regularly to write. Some days we find it far easier to do this, than others. This book is for those *other* days.

Acknowledgements

Firstly, I'd like to thank the members of the writers' circle I go to, who have endured many of my workshops. As many of them know, the idea behind this book began life as a motivational workshop for one of our January meetings. There's a fine line between motivating members and kicking them in the posterior, and there were times in the workshop when I wondered whether I'd crossed it. However, many kindly commented to me afterwards how beneficial they'd found the advice and exercises, so I resolved to give them a good kick up the rear end more frequently!

I'd also like to thank Diane Perry, Julie Phillips, Vivien Hampshire and Lynne Hackles for allowing me to mention times in their own writing lives, which have helped to illustrate points I wanted to make in this book.

Finally, I'd like to thank my writing students, many of whom have gone on to become good friends, as well as published writers. I know they find it difficult to understand why I'm just as excited as they are when they receive their first acceptance letter. Positivity though, is very infectious.

Thank you.

Simon Whaley

Introduction

New Start, New You, New Writer

This is not a *how to write* book – it's a *how to keep writing in order to achieve your writing dreams* book. It's for any writer who wants to achieve more. YOU CAN do it, if YOU really WANT to. Whether you want to see your name in print as the writer of a star letter in a magazine, enter a highly prestigious writing competition, or become a novelist, thinking positively *can* make a difference. Whatever your writing ambitions are, this book will help you to achieve YOUR dreams, but only if YOU are prepared to put in the effort. Why, though, should you listen to me?

I've written a bestselling book.

My first book, *100 Ways For A Dog To Train Its Human*, spent four weeks on the UK top-ten non-fiction paperback bestseller lists. It has gone on to sell over 220,000 copies. Was I lucky? Yes, there was an element of luck involved, but I firmly believe that I *created* the opportunity for that luck to come along and use. I was the person, after all, who wrote, rewrote (five times I'd like to point out), finished and submitted the book for publication in the first place. Its sales success was the icing on the cake. I did not set out to write a best-selling book, but I did set out to write a book. Since then, I've had eight more books published and have plenty more just waiting to be written!

I've had competition success.

I won first prize in the David Thomas Charitable Trust Writing Awards (*Writers' News magazine*) in April 1998 for a story called *Foggy Morning* and received an *Award for Excellence* from the

Outdoor Writers and Photographers Guild for a series of articles I wrote in a local magazine. The North American edition of my book, *100 Ways For A Dog To Train Its Human*, was nominated for excellence in the Dog Writers Association of America's Book Humor category.

I am a regularly published writer.

Several hundred of my articles have appeared in print and on the Internet. My short stories have been published in the UK, Ireland, Australia and New Zealand.

Since January 2004, I have been a full-time, freelance writer. Despite all of these achievements though, I am still a rejected writer. Sometimes, I am rejected several times a day.

Do I have a degree in writing? No. Did I get a good grade in my English O level? No. (I scraped through with a C grade, which in those days was the lowest pass.) Is my mother or father the head of a big publishing company? No. (More's the pity!) Do I have an agent? No. Not at the moment. I haven't needed one for my first nine books, but that doesn't mean to say that I won't have one in the future. My success so far has been achieved without one.

A POSITIVE WRITER IS A PRODUCTIVE WRITER. A PRODUCTIVE WRITER IS A SUCCESSFUL WRITER.

I believe my writing achievements are down to thinking as positively as I can at ALL times. Yes, I have days just like everyone else that could have gone better, although I try not to think of those as bad days. But, as a positive writer, I've learned to look on the bright side of my writing life. A positive writer IS a productive writer. A productive writer is more likely to become a published writer. Therefore a productive writer CAN become a successful writer. Positivity leads to higher productivity, which in turn increases the opportunity for success.

If you dream about being the next JK Rowling, Stephen King, Stephanie Myers, Thomas Keneally, Chetan Bhagat or Terry Pratchett then there's something you need to know. They didn't achieve it by dreaming. They did it by sitting down and producing written work. That means putting a bum on a chair and either picking up a pen and notebook, or caressing a keyboard with some fingers. And that means regularly. Ideally, it means EVERYDAY. But then, in your heart of hearts, you already knew that didn't you? There's more to putting your bum on a chair and writing though. You NEED to *believe* that you CAN achieve YOUR writing goals and that you WILL attain them. You MUST believe in YOURSELF.

And there's the important word. **Believe**. You have to believe that you can achieve what you want to achieve, because it isn't anyone else's job to do so. I've lost count how many workshops I've run where someone has come up to me and said, "Oh, I don't think I could ever write a book." And guess what? They haven't. Because that is what they believe. They believe they don't have the ability to write a book, when, in actual fact, they probably do. But because they don't believe they can write a book, they don't write a book. It's called the self-fulfilling prophecy. So, why not turn it around and make the self-fulfilling prophecy one that *will* work in your favour?

On average, more than 125,000 new books are published every year. We therefore know that it is possible for the human being to write a book. We also know that it is possible to get a book published. Those who have succeeded have believed they can do it.

The way to remain positive is to keep hold of your beliefs. Believe that you CAN do it and you are more likely to take the necessary steps required to ensure that you do reach your goal.

This book began life as a workshop I gave to the writers' group that I go to and afterwards many came up to me and said it was just what they needed – a great kick up the backside. In fact, one member later emailed me and said, *"Since your workshop I've set myself the target of writing 500 words a day, and I am achieving this. As a result, I've achieved over 12,000 words of my novel since our last group meeting. It's fantastic, I'm so overjoyed!"*

I also used my workshop as the basis for a blog posting and this generated a lot of positive feedback too. It was also picked up by an E-zine who wanted to use it as the main article for their next issue. They even paid me for it – how positive is that? So, being an optimistic writer, I realised that perhaps there was a book in this idea. And here it is.

You'll have noticed already that there are times when I have used CAPITALS to emphasize certain words. Now, I know that in the world of email etiquette, capitals are the equivalent of SHOUTING. I make no apologies for this. Sorry, I meant to say, I MAKE NO APOLOGIES FOR THIS! Why? Because there are times when we think we are listening, yet often we are only hearing what we want to hear. Until someone invents a book that can slap you across the face when it wants to ensure that you've understood an important point, this is the only method that I have available to me. Heck, if I want to slap you across the face with both hands, I may even **SHOUT IN BOLD!**

So, if you want to become a positively productive and successful writer, then turn the page and prepare to bend over. There's a foot heading for your rear end right now. **YOU CAN** do it if **YOU REALLY WANT** to!

Part I

Setting Achievable Writing Goals

Goals

Do you start each New Year with a long list of resolutions? How many of them harbour your writing dreams? What are YOUR writing dreams?

- ☺ To write a novel?
- ☺ To become a bestselling writer?
- ☺ To sell an idea to Hollywood and retire on the proceeds?

The problem with making big New Year resolutions is that they are too big to tackle on their own. When we sit down as writers, it is often the big dream we have at the forefront of our minds. If we think about setting ourselves a goal, we tend to set a whopping great big New Year's resolution of a goal, even if it's on a wet weekend in April. Have you ever set out to write a 100,000-word novel and two hours later, when all you have achieved are three measly paragraphs, found despondency setting in? Suddenly that 100,000th word seems completely unobtainable. The end is nowhere in sight. Do you close your notebook, never to look at those paragraphs again?

A JOURNEY OF A THOUSAND MILES BEGINS WITH ONE SMALL STEP

It was the Chinese Philosopher, Lao Tzu, who said that a journey of a thousand miles begins with one small step. It might sound corny. It may even come across as patronising. But don't dismiss it, because it IS true. Every 100,000-word novel begins with a first chapter. Every first chapter begins with an opening sentence, and every opening sentence begins with a first word. To remain positive on our journey to the realisation of our dreams, we need to break our trip down into those smaller steps. However, in order to make that first step, you need to know where YOUR journey is going to take YOU.

I hope the word *goal* doesn't frighten you. It shouldn't. Your goals should excite you. They're yours, after all! However, I'm aware that the setting of goals and targets are part and parcel of many people's ordinary and mundane work life. As someone who used to work for a major high street bank, I was always being set targets. The problem with these targets is that they were always someone else's figures. I wasn't asked how many credit cards I thought I could sell, I was told what my target was and that's what I had to aim for! Remember, when I talk about goals in this book, I'm referring to something that you dream of. This is something that you *want* to aim for. A writing goal is for YOU to set, nobody else. This is YOUR dream that you are striving towards.

Don't wait for January 1st!

You can start making your goals at ANY time. Start today! Start now!

Long-term

When you set yourself a goal, what you actually need to do is set yourself *three* types of goals – long-term, medium-term and short-term. Our long-term goals are those big New Year-type resolutions, but instead of thinking about them and setting them five minutes before the chimes of midnight, we need to be practical. We need to be REALISTIC. Which of the following are realistic goals?

- ☺ Selling a movie to Hollywood?
- ☺ Writing a bestselling book?
- ☺ Writing a novel?

Of the three goals listed above, the most realistically achievable is the third one – writing a novel. Why? Because it's the one goal that YOU have full control over. YOU CAN write a whole novel, if YOU make the commitment. Notice how the goal is to write a novel, not to have a novel published. To have a novel published requires other people (publishers or agents) to help you to achieve your goal. YOU are more likely to achieve YOUR goals if you have more opportunity to influence the outcome of your goal.

Once you've written a novel, that's the time to set yourself the new long-term goal of getting it published. Yes, you will need other people to help you with this, but there are steps you can take *when* you reach this moment. Part of that process will be to break this long-term goal down into more manageable stages, over which you have more control. Of course, achieving this new *to be published* goal is psychologically easier when you actually have a finished novel to send out to publishers in the first place!

How long is a long-term goal?

How long is a piece of string? Long-term goals are those bigger projects that take time to complete. They could be a few months, a few years or even longer. Think BIG and dream. Long-term goals need to stretch you. They won't be easily achievable, nor should they be. Nothing in life worth achieving is ever easy. They should challenge you and make you grow as a person and as a writer. If your long-term goal is easily achieved, then the only person you are fooling is yourself.

Medium-term

If a long-term goal is the destination of our journey, then our medium-term goals need to be the service station stops. Breaking goals down into smaller, manageable chunks helps us to remain focussed on the overall project, whilst also giving us the psychological boost of achieving something. Examine your writing goal and ask yourself how you can break it down into smaller targets. If, for example, your long-term goal was to enter a prestigious short story competition with a closing date in four months' time, your medium-term goals could be as follows:

☺ 3 months before the closing date – complete the first draft.

☺ 2 months before the closing date – complete editing the second draft.

☺ 1 month before the closing date – complete the final revision.

By following these medium-term goals and meeting every one of them, YOU WILL achieve your long-term goal of having an entry written and prepared in time for submission to the competition. Instead of sitting at your desk with pen and paper in hand trying to think of a perfect short story to write and send off in four months' time, you only need to think about completing the first draft in a month. This makes the job feel easier to tackle psychologically. You don't have to look quite so far ahead. Your immediate goal is nearer to you. As a result, it is more attainable. Psychologically, you'll be thinking, *this is something I CAN do.*

As a writing tutor, I've discovered that many new writers believe that what they write has to be perfect, highly-polished prose, immediately. They worry about every word as soon as they've written it and so they spend hours agonising over the first word. When the perfect sentence fails to materialise, they begin to doubt themselves and their ability. And so the negativity begins to grow. Perfection isn't created first time round. Perfection is honed. First drafts are not perfect. Accept that.

In my short story competition example, you know that your entry doesn't have to be perfect in a month's time, because you know that you've programmed other medium-term goals in the future to deal with perfecting your story. But once YOU have completed that first draft, you'll know that YOU ARE one step closer to achieving YOUR goal.

Remember – Rome wasn't built in a day!

(And you can take out the clichés when you edit your work.)

Short-term

Short-term goals are the immediate ones. They need to be the goals to aim for over the next few minutes, hours or days. Do you want to write 500 words before lunch? Perhaps you want to finish the first draft of an article by the end of the day, or complete the whole thing and send it off by the end of the week. Short-term goals are the stepping-stones that help you to achieve your medium-term goals. They are the important motorway junctions that lead you to the medium-term service stations. These are the goals that will make you feel pleased with yourself at the end of the day. They are the first steps on *your* great journey of a thousand miles.

Short-term goals need to be finely balanced. They should be attainable, but they should still force you to make a concerted effort in order to achieve them. There's no point in saying that you want to write 500 words before lunch, if you only achieve 300 words by the allotted time and decide to make lunchtime three hours later in the hope that you will have achieved 500 words by then! If you only have half an hour to go before lunch, and you're 200 words short, then push yourself to reach YOUR target. As I've already said, you can perfect the words later.

Example of long, medium and short-term goals

To enter a writing competition:

- The closing date is in four months' time. (**Long-term goal**)
  - First month – create a first draft. (**Medium-term goal**)
    - First week – outline story. (**Short-term goal**)
    - Second week – create character biographies. (**Short-term goal**)
    - Third week – finalise plot. (**Short-term goal**)
    - Fourth week – write first draft. (**Short-term goal**)
  - Second month – edit first draft. (**Medium-term goal**)
    - First week – put story aside. Don't look at it. (**Short-

term goal)
- Second week – review story. Edit text. **(Short-term goal)**
- Third week – put story aside. Don't look at it. **(Short-term goal)**
- Fourth week – review story. Edit text. **(Short-term goal)**
○ Third month – revise story to produce final draft. **(Medium-term goal)**
  - First week – put story aside. Don't look at it. **(Short-term goal)**
  - Second week – review story again. Read it aloud. **(Short-term goal)**
  - Third week – put story aside. Don't look at it. **(Short-term goal)**
  - Fourth week – final review and edit. **(Short-term goal)**
○ Fourth month – Submit story. **(Medium-term goal)**
  - First week – Check all competition rules. **(Short-term goal)**
  - Second week – Post entry allowing plenty of time before the final closing date. (Good luck!) **(Short-term goal)**

To write a novel:
- Write a 100,000-word novel in a year. **(Long-term goal)**
  ○ Write 8,334 (figure rounded) words every month. **(Medium-term goal)**
    - Write 274 (figure rounded) words every day. **(Short-term goal)**

To write more articles in the next year:
- Write 12 articles in a year. **(Long-term goal)**
  ○ Write one article every month. **(Medium-term goal)**
    - First week – research article topic. **(Short-term goal)**
    - Second week – devise article structure and write

opening paragraph. **(Short-term goal)**
- Third week – complete first draft. **(Short-term goal)**
- Fourth week – revise and edit article before submitting. **(Short-term goal)**

Take a look at the second example above – to complete a 100,000-word novel in a year. At first, that goal may seem daunting, especially if you've never written anything of this length before! I know. I've been there! However, the medium-term goal of a little over 8,000 words a month isn't quite as frightening. Break this down further into a short-term goal of 274 words a day, and suddenly the whole project looks achievable. That's when you realise that you CAN do this. And that's the point of this practical exercise. If writing a 100,000-word novel fills you with dread and panic, I guarantee YOU WILL FAIL. If you believe that you can't write a 100,000-word novel, YOU WILL FAIL. Whereas writing 274 words every day is much more attainable and easier to cope with mentally. And when you achieve your first 274 words, YOU WILL be proud that YOU HAVE achieved YOUR goal. If you continue to do this, by the end of the first month, YOU WILL have achieved your medium-term goal of over 8,000 words. Therefore, if you continue to achieve your daily short-term goal of 274 words for 365 days, by the end of the year, YOU WILL reach your goal of a 100,000-word novel. Congratulations. Celebrate. YOU deserve it!

*The more frequently you achieve your short-term goals, the easier it becomes to accept that YOU CAN do it. You will begin to **believe** in yourself. You'll then realise that your other long-term goals ARE achievable too, but only if you break them down into manageable targets.*

S.M.A.R.T.
When you've produced your own personal list of short, medium

and long-term goals, ask yourself whether they are S.M.A.R.T. enough. Don't panic, this doesn't mean that they have to be cleverer than you! However, to ensure that you can achieve them and, more importantly, know when you have achieved them, all of your goals need to meet the S.M.A.R.T. criteria. The acronym stands for:

☺ Specific
☺ Measurable
☺ Achievable
☺ Realistic
☺ Timely

SPECIFIC goals are clearly defined goals. *To write 100 words in an hour* is a specific goal. You know what you have to do and when you have to do it by. You will know when you have achieved your goal. Whereas, *to write some words*, isn't a precise goal. How many is *some*? When will you know that what you have written is enough?

MEASURABLE goals allow you to monitor your achievements so far. The specific goal above, *to write 100 words in an hour*, is measurable in two ways. Firstly, as you write, you can keep track of how many words you have written and secondly, you can measure how much time you have left to achieve the goal.

ACHIEVABLE goals are sensible goals. By this, I mean sensible when taking your current situation and circumstances into consideration. For example, writing 10,000 words in a day may be achievable if you have hired a log cabin on a remote island, miles away from any distractions, family members, friends, phones, emails etc. and you can spend 12 hours in front of your laptop, notebook or computer. It is not achievable if you have to take the kids to school, do the weekly shop, do a day's work, collect the kids from school, then feed and entertain them until they go to bed. The key to remaining positive is to understand your limitations and work your goals around them. If you can't achieve them, depression will quickly surround you like a fog. Suddenly, you'll start to believe that you will never be a writer. Don't let that happen.

REALISTIC goals are rational goals. Realistically, is your goal *to write a bestselling novel* achievable, if you haven't written anything longer than an irate email to your gas company? It's not impossible, but is it realistic? If you buy a ticket, it's not impossible that you will be this week's lucky jackpot winner on the lottery. People do win most weeks, don't they? But is it realistic? Is it likely to happen to you?

TIMELY goals are those that every professional writer has. They're called deadlines. Everything has to be achieved by a certain time. A deadline allows you to measure whether you have achieved what you set out to achieve. A goal with no timescale gives you no incentive to sit down and tackle it. That's why, as a positively productive writer, it's important to have a mixture of short, medium and long-term goals.

So, when you begin to create your list of goals ask yourself, are they S.M.A.R.T. ones? Do you know what you have to do and when you have to do it by? Do you think you can do it in the time you've set aside? If your family circumstances mean that you can only devote 30 minutes a day to your writing, then you need to know what your goal is for those 30 minutes. S.M.A.R.T. goals will help you to become a positively productive writer. Staying positive means being able to measure how far along your journey of a thousand miles you have travelled, and how much further there is still to go.

Which comes first – short or long?

It's imperative that you have a clear understanding of where your great writing journey is going to take you, and therefore the easiest way to devise your short and medium-term goals is to work backwards. For example, to achieve a 100,000-word novel in a year, divide the figure by 12 to get a monthly total (100,000 words ÷ 12 months = 8,333 words per month). Or you could divide this by 52 weeks to get a weekly total (100,000 ÷ 52 = 1,923). Or, you could divide it by 365 days to arrive at a daily total of 274.

If you begin by setting yourself short-term goals, without knowing what your long-term goal is, then you will have no idea where your journey will take you, or when you have actually reached the end of it. As my previous work colleagues always enjoyed saying, *"Any road will do if you don't know where you are going!"* You should therefore concentrate on creating short and medium-term goals that will help you to achieve your long-term goals. Know exactly where YOU want to go. This means goals designed by YOU, for YOU to get more of YOUR work written and submitted.

START NOW. Come on! To reach your long-term goal of becoming a positively productive writer you don't need any specialist equipment. Start a new document on your computer, or get a small index card and create a table or divide it into three columns. Label each column – long, medium and short. Now create and list YOUR goals. The first short-term goal is easy. In fact, write it down now. It is:

> *To create a series of short, medium and long-term goals*

Then, as soon as you have created your goals, you can tick this one off and already you've taken that first step! Well done. See? It's easy when you know how, isn't it?

Writing down your goals like this also makes them clearer in your mind. This may seem strange, but seeing something in black and white helps the brain to focus on what it is we want to achieve. The art of committing something to paper suggests that we are making a *commitment*. Writing it down formalises that commitment. Suddenly, it's there for all to see. This takes us one step closer to turning them into reality.

"A goal is nothing more than a dream with a deadline."
Joe L Griffith

Reviewing Goals

Learn to review your goals on a regular basis. How are you doing? If you're doing well and meeting all of your short-term goals without difficulty, are they TOO easy for you? Do you need to stretch yourself a little more? If you're achieving 500 words during your allotted writing time, why not try to write 750 words instead? It is important that we continue to develop and stretch ourselves. Goals should be challenging. This is because sometimes we will stretch a goal in order to make it fit the timescale available. For example, if your target is to complete a short story by the end of the day, and you sense that you will definitely achieve this, you will relax. I know, because I've fallen into this trap!

Parkinson's Law

It was C Northcote Parkinson, Professor of History at the University of Singapore, who opened an article in The Economist in 1955 with the sentence:

"It is a commonplace observation that work expands so as to fill the time available for its completion."

Blast! We've been sussed again then, haven't we?

It happens to all of us. You will slow down, but only enough to ensure that you still meet your target. Yet that's all. You won't achieve anything *extra*. If you find yourself achieving a goal earlier than planned, consider setting yourself another short-term goal, just to push yourself that bit further. What about writing a letter to a magazine's letter page if you finish that short story early? Stretching yourself that little bit more could see a new idea generated, a short letter published, or an outline for an article or short story. Use your goals to maximise your writing time.

Of course, life doesn't always go to plan; so if things are going badly, are you being too difficult on yourself? Have you experienced a change in your circumstances that is making your writing life challenging? One of the complications we writers face is that life has a habit of getting in our way. DON'T let that be an excuse for underachieving, but understand and accept that what was possible last week MAY NOT be possible this week. If next week looks as though it will be a little easier for you, then it would be sensible to reduce your short-term goals for this week and then increase them next week to compensate. That way, you are acknowledging that life is getting in the way, but you are still setting yourself some goals to aim for and meet on a daily basis. Adjusting your goals like this means that you are still aware of your medium-term goals too. Psychologically, to stay positive and ultimately productive, you need goals that ARE achievable every day. You need to believe that you CAN achieve them.

Only you can decide the best way to review your goals. Going back to our example of a 100,000-word novel in a year, I calculated that it's possible to achieve this by writing 274 words a day. However, if after a couple of weeks you find yourself writing 500 words in a day, what should you do? Should you change your goal from 274 words a day to 500 and finish the novel early, or should you stop writing at 274 words, and do some other writing in the allotted time instead?

Personally, if I were producing 500 words a day when my original goal was 274, I would continue writing 500 words a day. If my brain has become used to producing this volume (more about this in Part III), then I'm not going to fight it. I would amend my short-term goal from 274 words to 500 words. However, I would NOT amend my long-term goal target date of the end of the year.

By their very nature, long-term goals are some way off in the distance. No one knows what lies around the next corner. Family bereavements, personal accidents, flood, pestilence, war; who knows what could happen? It is far better psychologically, to achieve a long-term goal early because you were exceeding your short and medium-term goals, than it is to bring a long-term goal forward, fail to meet it and then have to reset it somewhere in the future again. It will feel like a setback and, as positively productive writers, we want to reduce negative experiences!

Likewise, if your goal is to write 500 words in a day and, for some unknown reason, you sit down and six hours later suddenly find that you've added 5,000 words to your manuscript, DO NOT THINK THAT YOU CAN TAKE THE NEXT NINE DAYS OFF! You can't. You MUST sit down tomorrow and write your next 500 words. Why? Because tomorrow's 500 words will be some of the hardest you will ever write. All you will be thinking about is yesterday's amazing achievement. Thirty minutes in and suddenly, you'll realise that you haven't written a word and that's when your brain starts panicking. If 5,000 words came so easily yesterday, then why can't I do it today? What's wrong with me? And if 500 words are so difficult the day after, just think how impossible they would be if you left them for another *nine* days before trying. It will be hard work, but you MUST persevere.

If it's flowing, keep it going!
If your writing is going well, don't stop until you REALLY have to. Days like this don't come often!

The true sign of success is when you are busy creating new long-term goals to replace those YOU have already ACHIEVED. In theory, you will never achieve everything you set out to attain (because there's always something new to aim for!). However, looking back on all of your achievements completed to date will provide a huge sense of satisfaction, which certainly makes up for it!

Reviewing your goals also means creating new long-term

goals as they become appropriate. For example, I mentioned earlier that when you have written and completed your novel, that's the time to set yourself the goal of getting it published. One of my first long-term goals was to have a book published. When I achieved this, I changed it to getting five books published. Now I've achieved this, I've changed it to getting ten books published. (And this is book ten, so I'll have to change this long-term goal again soon.)

To remain positive, you always need to have something to aim for. You must have a reason for getting up in the morning, or to use those precious 30 minutes a day that you have carefully created for yourself, in order to write. To succeed as a positively productive writer you MUST be self-disciplined with your writing time, and goals will help you to create that self-discipline. As a full-time writer, I'm continuously devising new goals for myself. Despite paying into a personal pension plan, I can never see myself actually retiring from writing!

Postponing goals

Are there ever occasions when you should postpone your goals? Yes. But do not treat this as your get-out-of-jail-free card. If you do, it is only you who is losing out in the end isn't it?

Life has a habit of throwing things at us when we're not looking. There are accidents, bereavements, illnesses and feuds, which all take up time when we could be writing. It's necessary to be flexible in circumstances like that. Sometimes it is still possible to make a token effort towards your goals when fate tries to divert your journey. During the writing of this book, a family member spent over eight weeks in hospital, which meant I had to curtail my writing time during the day to enable me to make hospital visits on a daily basis. I had to amend my goals accordingly. But I still used the half hour journey travelling to the hospital and back to think of ideas, mull them over and find solutions to my writing problems. I'd often spend a couple of minutes at the end of my journey jotting down my thoughts. I adapted to my current situation.

One of the great joys of writing is that you never know where it may lead. And this guides us to another situation where it may be necessary to amend your goals. Sometimes, an opportunity arises that is just too good to turn away.

Later, I shall tell you about a writing friend, Diane Perry, who wrote a book called *100 Ways For A Chicken To Train Its Human* (Hodder & Stoughton, ISBN: 9780340910207). Now, Diane enjoys writing articles, but her goal has always been to write children's novels. And this is what she does when she's not working at her full-time civil service job. But one day, I suggested the idea for *100 Ways For A Chicken To Train Its Human* (after my own dog version), and she put her children's novel on the backburner to concentrate on this project. It was necessary to tackle this whilst the idea was new and the publishers were still developing the 100 Ways series. So she did. Was she right to do so? Yes, because she was still writing – albeit on a different project. Her reward was that the book was published. And now she has completed her children's novel too. She didn't forget her original goal, she merely postponed it to maximise this new writing opportunity.

One of the magazines that I do a lot of work for has asked me to do several other features in preparation for next year's issues. The problem with articles is that you need to prepare them months in advance, and if you need pictures, you need them to be appropriate. I'm often writing an article for June in February, but the trouble with the photographs I take in February is that they are not very June-like! So, the editor asked me to attend a series of events recently, which I could take pictures of and then write up the articles at my leisure in readiness for next year.

As a freelance writer, one of my goals is to spend some of my time writing query letters to editors trying to generate work. During this period, though, I had to postpone this goal whilst I worked on these other articles for following year. But this was acceptable to me because I was still writing.

If ever you're unsure about whether it is right to postpone a goal, ask yourself the following question:

Will postponing one goal still enable me to develop as a writer?

In the examples I've given above, postponement of a goal has enabled both Diane and I to achieve other writing goals. It's that which makes the decision the right one at that particular time. Maximise your opportunities, don't waste them.

Rewards

This is the best bit! Think of this as your own employee bonus system. Reward YOURSELF for achieving YOUR goals. YOU deserve it! So, if you've set yourself a target of writing 1,000 words in a day and YOU ACHIEVE it, reward yourself. Cook yourself something nice for an evening meal. If you achieve 1,200 words by lunchtime, then meet up with a friend. And if they buy lunch, even better!

Make sure that the reward is appropriate for the goal achievement. Attaining the completion of a first draft of a short story is not the time to go and treat yourself to a new car! Wait until you've won the prestigious competition, or sold a novel. But, you MUST reward yourself for EVERY goal you achieve. These rewards are the incentives that ensure you keep going back to your desk and having another go tomorrow. They are the proof that you are achieving YOUR goals.

We all have different interests in life, so no two writers' rewards will be the same. However, *you* know what *your* little weaknesses are. Chocolate? An extra glass of wine? Internet chat forums. Well, here's your chance to give yourself a valid reason for indulging in them. But ONLY if you achieve what you set out to achieve. Yes, used properly, your weaknesses can help you to achieve your writing dreams!

You could set yourself another short-term goal of listing as many rewards as you can think of, and then deciding which ones would be suitable incentives for meeting your short, medium and long-term goals. Of course, when you've done this, you should then remunerate yourself with an appropriate short-term goal reward. Now, which one will it be?

Example rewards

Long-term rewards could include:

- Having a holiday! A weekend break, or something longer if you've completed a large project.
- Treat yourself to a new toy: a computer gadget, camera, MP3 player, new curling tongs, new chair for your writing desk. (See The Write Place in Part III for more ideas here.)
- A spa break with friends.

Medium-term rewards could include:

- Book yourself a massage or beauty treatment.
- Go on a girlie shopping trip with friends.
- Have a game of golf with your mates.
- Have a fun day out with the family, away from your desk.

Short-term rewards could include:

- Surfing the Internet for 10 minutes.
- Having a chat on the phone with a friend.
- Buying a new music track for your MP3 player.
- Having a piece of cake, or chocolate.
- Enjoying a glass of wine at the end of the day.
- Meeting up with friends in the evening.

And when you achieve one of your really big, humongous, New Year's resolutions of a goal, do something really big and humongous to reward yourself! Celebrate in style. When my first book sold 100,000 copies in its first three months, I did something really big to celebrate. I resigned from my day job. Now, I wouldn't recommend this to everyone, but it had always been one of my long-term goals to become a full-time writer. I did have other freelance work lined up and the large sales figures of the first book certainly helped cushion me financially for the first few months! Living my life without giving myself the chance to be a full-time freelance writer would have left me with regrets. I don't want to put too blunt a point on it, but we are only on this planet once and positively productive writers don't have time for negative regrets! Which of the following is worse?

☺ Lying on your deathbed wishing you'd found the time to write your book, play, or movie?

☺ Or lying on your deathbed, wishing you'd dusted your ornaments more frequently?

A Writing Buddy

For the reward system to work, you need to be self-disciplined. Most writers show some signs of self-discipline otherwise nothing would get written in the first place! However, if you're reading this book and planning to use the techniques to improve your own productivity, then it's going to involve some changes to your previous routine. Managing this change may not be easy to begin with and this is where it can be useful to have a Writing Buddy.

A Writing Buddy is someone who will encourage you to press on when your motivation dips. They don't need to live locally, or even in the same country. A Buddy simply needs to be someone whom you can contact easily on a regular basis. Email or phone will suffice, but if you know someone locally and can meet up regularly, then that's great too. The important point is that your Buddy will be an external control; someone who knows what *your* goals are and can keep you focussed on achieving them. If, for example, you've set yourself a target of writing 1,000 words every day, then tell your writing buddy. And then email them with your total word count at the *end of every day*. Knowing that you have to declare your achievements to a third party can provide that extra spur you need when your spirits start flagging at 800 words.

It works both ways, so a good Buddy is someone who is also a writer. Be a Buddy to your Buddy. Be there to support them in the same way that they help you and together you can both increase your productivity. And share some of your rewards with your Buddy too! Agree to meet up for lunch when you've both achieved a significant medium-term goal, for example. It's only right that you share the fun, as well as the torment! Writing can feel a solitary activity, but a Buddy can remove that isolation.

If you are a writer who likes to work on several projects, you might find it beneficial to have a Buddy for each type of project. For example, have a different Buddy for short stories, novels and articles. If ever you get stuck on a project, it can be useful to chat about your difficulties with another writer who understands those difficulties. A poet may not understand the challenges that a short story writer faces, so it may take another short story writer to help put things into perspective for you.

However you decide to develop your Buddy system, make sure it is someone you can contact easily. In Part III, we'll look at the support writers' circles can offer, although, they may only meet monthly or fortnightly. Your Buddy needs to be someone you can contact between those meetings, because if you have to wait two weeks for someone to give you a kick up the rear end, it may need to be a really painful kick to get you started again!

Part II

Learn To Look On The Bright Side Of Life

Twisting Negatives Into Positives

So, you've set out what your short, medium and long-term goals are and you know how you are going to reward yourself when you achieve them. Congratulations! You have already taken several steps along your journey of a thousand miles. Now it's time to find out how to survive when things go wrong. Because they will.

Every negative has a positive. Don't believe me? Well go to your MP3 player, digital camera or television remote control and take out the battery. There. See? Negative at one end... and positive at the other.

So, is your toner or ink jet cartridge half-full or half-empty? Are you the type of person whose cup is either half-full or half-empty? (Mine is always half-full... unless it is a cup of tea when it will always be empty.) Our outlook on life can be so influential in what we achieve. Did you know that we are not born as optimists or pessimists? It's a character trait that we learn. If you're a pessimist, that's good news, because it means that you can learn to be an optimist!

As a freelance writer, I am a failure every day and often, *several times* a day. If I send out ten query emails to editors, pitching article ideas for their magazines, Murphy's Law says I'll get eleven rejections. Ten will be from today's mail out, the other one left over from yesterday. Yet I accept it isn't *me personally* being rejected. It is just *that particular* idea at *that particular* time.

Getting a rejection hurts and rightly so. As writers, we've either had to spend time finishing a complete piece of work, or we've had to develop several ideas in the hope that an editor will be interested in one of them. Being told, *"No, not for us I'm afraid,"* is demoralising, particularly when you're reliant on selling words in order to put food on the table. It can also be disheartening if your writing time is limited each week. Spending your precious 30 minutes a day for two weeks working on a short story, only to have it rejected, will hurt. That's when you start wondering, would that time have been better spent working on something else? I don't believe so. In my opinion, everything you write helps you to develop further as a writer. In this game, nothing is wasted. What is rejected today can be sold tomorrow. So, learn to twist it around.

TURN THAT BATTERY UPSIDE DOWN AND LOOK AT THE POSITIVE END.

When you first receive the rejection, **IGNORE IT**. I know, it's difficult, but you must. Why? Because you're emotionally hurt. Whenever we write something, we always dream of acceptance, publication and being rewarded financially too. Rejection means we now have to come to terms with the fact that those dreams have not come true at this particular moment in time. But here's another reason for ignoring the rejection. Did you know that rejection temporarily lowers our IQ (Intelligence Quotient) level? So, when we are rejected, we don't have the brainpower to make a rational and intelligent decision about what to do with our manuscript. (Although I'm sure many writers know exactly where they would like to shove their rejected words!)

You need to learn how to lick your emotional wounds and believe in yourself again. Getting eleven rejections on the same day is tough. However, I actually see it as a positive event because I'm dead chuffed that I've had ten ideas in the first place to send out. And getting all of the editors to reply to my pitches is actually a pretty amazing achievement in itself! Many don't even bother replying at all if the idea doesn't excite them.

It also means that ten editors have come across my name today. Just because they didn't like today's idea, that doesn't mean to say that they will reject tomorrow's. However, because they rejected me today, when my name pops up tomorrow, they may even remember it. A writer who continues to submit ideas to an editor, who rejects them, shows determination. Editors do take note of this. One day, one of your ideas WILL be the perfect pitch and the editor WILL be intrigued. The fact that you've continued to bombard him or her with your *appropriate* ideas (note that the ideas must be appropriate for that particular editor!), and not been put off by their rejections, demonstrates a level of professionalism. It may be enough to give them the confidence to trust you with an assignment. I've had an editor reject an idea I sent them one day, only for them to contact me the next with a commission on an entirely different topic. Would that positive outcome have happened if I hadn't gone to the trouble of approaching the editor the previous day with an idea? This proves that all of those other rejections were not a waste of time. They led to a positive outcome.

Think like a salesperson. Why? Because they're brilliant at focussing on the positive aspects of something and ignoring the negatives! The next time you receive a rejection, look at it like a salesperson would. They may sell you this 'rejection situation' by saying that you now have:

☺ *A new opportunity to review and improve your text.*
☺ *A new opportunity to offer your work elsewhere.*
☺ *An opportunity to send your work to a higher paying market. (That's happened to me a couple of times. I've initially targeted a magazine where I knew their rates of pay, only to have it rejected. I rewrote and resubmitted the piece to a second market, to find that not only did they accept it, but they also paid more money than my first target market!)*

The Truth Behind Rejection

I accept that rejection isn't personal, because I can prove it. I once wrote an article about Norfolk's heritage coastline. I targeted the local county magazine, *Norfolk Journal*, wrote my article with their readers in mind and sent it off. It came back rejected. At the time, I didn't know of any other suitable magazines in Norfolk that I could rework my material for, so I put it to one side. About a year later, I read in one of the writing magazines that the *Norfolk Journal* had a new editor. So, I printed out a fresh copy, popped it in the post, and awaited the response. It came back rejected.

Sometime later, I heard that the magazine had yet another new editor (presumably the previous two had been washed out to sea!), so once again I printed off a fresh copy and sent it out. That editor ACCEPTED it, despite it being word for word exactly the same as my previous two submissions. See what I mean? My work hadn't been rejected because it was unsuitable, poorly written, or targeted at the wrong market. It may have been a question of timing. Perhaps the previous editors had recently accepted material on a similar topic (something I wouldn't have been aware of). Or perhaps they simply got out of bed on the wrong side on the mornings that my submissions arrived. (I know which scenario I believe in.) However, the important point to make here is that both of those first editors felt that my work wasn't right for them at that particular time. They were not telling me to give up writing and take up a peacekeeping role in some far away war zone instead!

Editors make mistakes. They are only human. Publishing is a fickle industry. There is no formula to guaranteed success. Just ask the publishers who rejected JK Rowling's Harry Potter and Frederick Forsyth's The Day of the Jackal. Neither author gave up after the first few rejections. As the inventor Thomas Edison said, "Many of life's failures are people who did not realize how close they were to success when they gave up." So, don't give up too early. In fact, don't give up at all. You may just be about to succeed.

To re-enforce this message, there's another example I want tell you about. I have sold an article to the very same editor, at the very same magazine, who'd rejected the very same article ten years previously! Again, I hadn't changed a single word. In my opinion, my writing was of a high enough standard, it was targeted at the right magazine and it was written with the right readership in mind. I suspect that it was rejected originally because an article written by another writer on the same subject appeared in the following issue. The editor clearly couldn't cover the same topic again in the immediate future and therefore he had no choice but to return my work. This was compounded by the fact that the magazine was a quarterly publication. With only four issues a year, a long time has to pass before the readers are willing to read something else on a similar subject. Ten years was a long wait... but it paid off in the end. The positive attitude in my mind likes to tell me that I was ten years ahead of my time! I can live with that. But, remember what I said earlier. Nothing in this writing game need ever be wasted. You CAN do it, if you persevere. Today's rejection can become tomorrow's acceptance.

Learning from rejection

Another way of coping with rejection is to twist it into a positive learning opportunity. A mistake is only a mistake if you make it again. If you keep repeating the same action, then you'll get the same result. (If you only write horror short stories and send them to a magazine that only prints romantic tales, you will always be rejected. The result will be the same, time and time again. But, if you change your action and send your horror stories to a market that publishes horror, then you have an opportunity to change the result. It *could* get accepted.) If you make a mistake once, but learn from it, YOU WILL be a better writer for it. Analyse every rejection for clues.

Rejection is just a stepping stone to success!

Firstly, if an editor gives ANY hint at all in the rejection letter, then take it on board. Editors are not there to provide a free critique service, so if their rejection letter contains any nugget of information, treat it like gold dust and learn from it. They have gone out of THEIR way to give YOU this piece of advice. They don't give guidance to every writer who submits work; only to those who they think show promise. That makes YOU SPECIAL!

Many rejection letters are standard, photocopied forms, but even if you get one of these don't dismiss the learning opportunity just yet. I once sent a short story to a magazine and it was rejected. It had a standard rejection letter with it, so at the time I just filed the paperwork to one side, deciding to look at it later with a view to rewriting it then. When I came to re-read it, I shouted out in shock when I turned to the last page of the story. There, on a pink sticky note, the editor had handwritten the comments, *"Simon, I like this but the twist at the end lets it down. Our guidelines say 'imagine it as a film – would the twist still work?' Is there any other development possible?"*

Wow! It's not often that such personal feedback is provided, but I took it on board. I rewrote the story with a different ending, ensuring that the twist would still work if my story were a film, and guess what? I sold that revised story. Not to the editor who'd rejected it, it turns out. She said my story was much better, but she just didn't like the new ending! But that didn't put me off. I sent the *improved* story to another magazine, which accepted it. How positive was the result from that initial rejection then? (Incidentally, writing stories with a twist that would work as a film means that the twist arises from the story itself. If the twist wouldn't work in a film, this suggests that the writer is concealing something from the reader, which they could quite easily see if they were watching the story as a film.)

Last week, a short story of mine was returned by a magazine with a standard rejection letter. When I quickly glanced through the manuscript (looking for any sticky notes!) something didn't seem quite right, yet I couldn't work out what. Scrutinising the paperwork more closely later on, I realised that this was not my *original* manuscript. This was a photocopy. Now, although I can't be sure, being a positive writer I'd like to think that this story got through the initial sift. Perhaps my story was photocopied for other magazine staff to read and pass judgement on, because it showed promise. One fact I do know is that according to my own records this magazine has taken eight weeks to reject my stories in the past. This one took twice as long to come back. Again, I could be wrong. It may have been delayed because it fell down the back of someone's desk, but that doesn't explain why it was photocopied. So, thinking positively, I felt that this rejection had some hope behind it. My story wasn't quite right but I was getting closer. It inspired me to have another go at writing a story for this publication.

That was rejected too. But this next rejection letter was different. It said:

> *Thank you for sending us your short story. Unfortunately it isn't what we are looking for at the moment, however, we enjoyed reading it and liked its style. Please do send us some more of your work.*

Now, I don't know about you, but I think that's a pretty positive rejection letter!

Lynne Hackles is a successful short story writer whose work has appeared in magazines in several countries including the UK and Australia. She's had stories rejected by a magazine that had marked up her manuscript with details of which issue they were scheduled to appear in and how many pages they were going to take up! See what I mean? Those rejections had nothing to do with the quality of the writing, did they? The magazine was all geared up to publishing the story but, for some reason best known to the magazine, it was rejected at this late production stage. But that's not the end of the story, because Lynne's often sold these stories to the very same magazine, a few years later, just like my article examples above. This tenacity is important.

Positive writers are tenacious writers!

Here's another tenacious example Lynne provided. "The year after I taught short story writing at Caerleon [see section on workshops, seminars and holidays], half a dozen people complained to me that they'd done everything I told them and their story had been rejected. The next person came up and said, 'I did everything you told me, and I've sold nineteen stories since this time last year.' She was the positive one who kept sending them out."

Notice how the first people to complain to Lynne spoke in the singular. They'd written *one* story and *it* had been rejected. The last writer had written several and found success with nineteen of them. You cannot let rejection stop you from writing. In fact, rejection should be the spur that keeps you going. Reject rejection!

Sometimes spotting the clues as to why a piece has been rejected isn't always easy. My previous article examples demonstrate that editors are *forced* to reject material that covers subjects they've just published or commissioned pieces for. This isn't always obvious until you see a future issue of the magazine. And before some of you start thinking that the editors are stealing ideas, let me quash that notion immediately. Banish those negative thoughts from your mind now!

It is common for writers to have similar ideas, particularly where anniversaries or seasonal hooks are involved. It seems that the bigger the anniversary, the more writers there are who write about it. I know because as a writing tutor I regularly read several of them myself. Many fiction writers will have a go at writing a story with a Christmas, Valentine's Day, Father's Day or Armistice Day theme at some point. Don't imagine that your ideas are being stolen, because they're not. Think positively.

Remember – turn that battery upside down and look for the positive. Be proud of the fact that you're obviously thinking on the same wavelengths as all of those other professional, published writers!

When we're starting out on our writing journeys, we assume that rejection is because there is something wrong with our writing. This is usually despite the rejection letter mentioning absolutely nothing about the quality of our writing! Negative writers tend to assume *the worst*, (due to their creative imaginations – more of which, later) yet rejection can be for any number of reasons, including:

- ☺ A magazine is fully stocked with material for the foreseeable future.
- ☺ An editor may have commissioned another writer to tackle a similar idea.
- ☺ A new editor has arrived and plans a new look with differently slanted material.
- ☺ Your target fiction magazine no longer needs Tale with a Twist stories, but Romance instead.
- ☺ The publisher believes the market is saturated with historical romance novels at present.
- ☺ Commissioned work will always take precedence over material submitted on spec, (even if your 'on spec' submission is of a higher quality).
- ☺ The editor is having a bad day. (Raging toothache, the kids

played up on the way to school this morning, the mother-in-law is coming round for tea tonight and guess who forgot to put the rubbish bins out this morning?)

Don't let an editor's negative mood affect your positive mood! Don't be scared of rejection. Some novice writers don't send out any of their work. Logically, if they never post anything off, they can never be rejected, can they? They think they are protecting themselves from the pain of rejection. That is the WRONG ATTITUDE! How do they know that it *will* be rejected? Their work may be accepted, but until they send it out there, they will never find out. The ONE person preventing them from being published is *them*, not anyone else. To be a writer, YOU need to BELIEVE that YOU are a writer.

Rejection holds nothing to be afraid of. Instead, embrace it with open arms. We NEED to be rejected. Whenever one of my submissions is rejected, I look at it again. How can I improve it? Nine times out of ten, I can. Importantly, rejections enable us to put a value on acceptance and success. The taste of success is so much sweeter when we've also had to swallow the bitter pill of rejection. I recently sold an article that I first wrote over eleven years ago. Fifteen times it had been rejected and rewritten to suit the readership of a different magazine. Yet finally, it was accepted. There were lots of bitter pills to swallow there, but when success came, boy was that sweet!

One of my students forwarded to me their very first rejection they had received. Rather stoically, they took it on the chin and said that they'd keep sending out work out to other editors. Great! I like my students to keep trying and accept that rejection is just part of being a writer. I was just about to email back saying this, when I scrutinised the rejection letter a little closer. This is what it said:

"I've had a look through your piece and while it sounds like a fasci-

nating trip, I don't think it fits with any of our plans for the upcoming months.

However, as it sounds like you've had some great experiences, I wondered if you'd like to get involved in the magazine in other ways – i.e. sending tips, advice and recommendations for our tips pages. I'd love to hear any you may have with a view to possibly including them in the magazine."

Er... hello? Where exactly is the *"go away and never darken my in-tray with your writing ever again"* comment? Yes, the editor has rejected the piece my student had submitted, but they are also asking to see *more* of my student's work! Now, admittedly, this wasn't the outcome my student was looking for, but the editor is still asking my student to send in more material. As rejection letters go, this is a pretty good one to get!

Sometimes, we become so focussed on the outcome *we wanted* from our submission that we become blind to any other opportunities that may be on offer from a publication or publisher.

Reviewing Your Work

The temptation to send out something as soon as you have finished it is immensely high, but don't do it. Instead, put your work to one side and enjoy the elation at having completed a project. Be proud of YOUR achievement. You have, after all, just taken yet another positive step in your journey. If you've taken on board my earlier comments about setting goals for yourself, this moment should represent one of those goals. You can only send out a project when you have completed it. Take a break at this stage and go and enjoy the reward that you have allocated for this success.

Take a break

Tempting though it may be, try to avoid looking at your finished piece of work again during your current writing period. Leave it for 24 hours *at least*. If you can leave it longer, even better. For me, the bigger the project is, the longer I leave it. Give it a try.

When you come back to look at your text again, you may be disheartened by what you see. Suddenly, all the mistakes become obvious. The typing errors become apparent, the inappropriate words that the spellchecker did not pick up will jump out and you may even spot sections where whole words are missing! Don't be disheartened – that's negative! Instead, be pleased with yourself. Not because you've made all of these mistakes, but because you HAVE spotted them. You now have the opportunity to improve your text, before sending it off. How does it feel, knowing that you could have submitted this inferior piece of work, whilst the euphoria of actually finishing it was encouraging you to send it off? Had you done so, then an editor could have seen all of these mistakes that you've now identified. Phew! And whilst an editor's job is to *edit*, they expect submissions to be as error free as possible.

So, here's the positive bit. This is where you CAN do something about those minor errors and rectify them all. Make the corrections and then, when you are ready to submit the piece, you will do so with confidence. Every time you make any changes to a piece of work, put it aside again to review later when your eyes are fresh. Only when you read a piece and make no further grammatical changes is it ready for submission.

Don't let this become an excuse not to send something off. Once you've caught all the spelling and typographical errors and checked your facts are correct, be brave – send it off. Don't keep titivating with it. **SEND IT OFF** *and get cracking on your next idea straight away!*

Read it out aloud

When re-reading your work, do something different and read it out aloud. There are many times when I have done this and felt a fool, (usually when I've been standing by an open window as someone has walked past, or when family members are in adjacent rooms) but do persevere. It works.

I have a tendency to write long sentences. (You've probably spotted this already, although, if I've revised this book properly, you won't have encountered too many!) Reading it out aloud helps me to spot these long sentences. Whenever I'm speaking my text, if I stumble, notice a word repetition, or stop to draw for breath, then I know that the text needs changing. It needs improving.

Why does this exercise work? All too often when we read quietly to ourselves, particularly when we are reading our own work, we *know* what comes next. We wrote it after all! And because of that, that's what our eyes *believe* is on the page, and that's what they *see*, even if that isn't what is on the page. When you read work out aloud, your brain has to work differently, because it needs to read exactly what is written and then instruct your mouth to say it. As a result, reciting your work out aloud forces you to read it differently – properly.

If a piece of text is easy to say out aloud, then it is also easy to read. Readers will react positively to your text, because you are making their job easier for them.

Getting feedback

In Part III of this book, I will suggest ways you can network with other writers that will enable you to obtain some feedback on your work. Getting others to read your writing, before you send it out to your intended market, can be useful. You should choose your reviewer carefully though.

Unless there is a specific reason for doing so, avoid asking family members. Criticism needs to be constructive. Relations have a habit of reading your work and saying, *"Yes, that's really good,"* if they think that's what you want to hear. Likewise, friends may be just as encouraging because they don't want to offend you. If there's a flaw in your text and they haven't told you about it, then asking them for their opinion and feedback has not been a productive exercise.

This is a great reason for joining a writers' circle. Here you can ask another writer for constructive feedback. For criticism to be constructive, it needs to have three elements:

- ☺ A clear explanation of *what* is wrong,
- ☺ An understanding of *why* it is wrong,
- ☺ And practical advice on *what action* you need to take to improve it.

If someone reads a short story you have written and says, *"No, that's awful,"* you have not been given any practical information. That's not criticism, that's personal opinion. However, if someone says, *"Your second paragraph doesn't work because you have too many adverbs in it, which slows down the pace of your story,"* then you have something practical to work on. This constructive advice tells you what is wrong (too many adverbs), why it is wrong (it slows down the pace), and what action you need to take to improve it (deleting the adverbs).

Asking for constructive criticism is a very positive step. The physical aspect of letting go and giving your work to someone else to read will make sending it to a complete stranger (an editor or a competition judge) much easier. It also demonstrates that you are willing to learn. Being prepared to take advice and learn from your mistakes shows maturity. You want your work to be the best it can be before you send it off. That's a professional attitude to have and that's positive!

However, the drawback with asking several members of a writers' circle to give you feedback is that you could be deluged with several different pieces of advice. Here's how to make the critiquing experience more positive and productive for you:

☺ If you're going to read your work out to a group of people, practise reading it out aloud at home in private first. It's important that you have confidence in what you are going to read out. Reading it aloud for the first time in front of a group of people, such as a writers' group, means that when you spot any mistakes (which you will), you are going to start feeling negative. You'll start apologising and then you'll begin stumbling because you're trying to make a mental note for later of what you need to change. As a result your recital will lose its impact. Several stop/starts during your reading will make it more difficult for your listeners to follow. This may hinder them giving you useful feedback, whilst also magnifying your own negative insecurities as you continue to read.

☺ Stand up when you read work out aloud, whether it is in your own writing space or in front of a group of people. It helps you to fill your lungs and use them to their full capacity. Being able to breathe properly makes the physical effort of speaking easier.

☺ Never begin saying, *"This is only a first draft, so I know it isn't very good."* Have confidence in what you have written! I hear this so many times at writers' circles. **DON'T BE NEGATIVE!**

☺ When you have finished, sit down and pick up a pen and paper. Write down EVERYTHING that is said. The physical act of committing all of these comments to paper helps your brain to retain the information and it also gives you something to do! This is important because if you are concentrating on writing down the feedback, you are less likely to respond verbally to the points that people are making. You won't then fall into the negative trap of *defending* your material. Reading out something that is personal to you can make you protective and that's not what constructive criticism is about. Listening to what is being said and then writing it down is a positive action. Defending your work with phrases like, *"No you don't understand, what I meant there was... "* is negative. If the listener hasn't understood what you were trying to say, that isn't their fault, it's yours. You haven't communicated your message clearly enough. So, use THEIR comments to help you make the improvements to YOUR text.

☺ Be proactive in your feedback. Before anyone starts giving you feedback, take control of the situation yourself. Start off by seeking positive feedback. Train your reviewers to be positive too. Ask positive questions like, *"What bits did you enjoy, and why?"* or *"What worked well for you and why?"* It's good to have other people reinforce what you have done right. If you have used a technique well, you may want to use the technique again in your writing. Try to ask reviewers for more positive comments than negative ones. The rule of three usually works well. Ask reviewers for one positive comment, one constructive comment about something that can be improved and then finish on another positive comment.

☺ Review the comments at home in your own writing space. Which pieces of advice you decide to act upon is entirely up to YOU. If one person has made a suggestion and you don't agree with it, then it's YOUR decision whether you do anything about it. If several people have raised the same comment, then you would probably be foolish to ignore it.

The right people's feedback

If your project is on a specialist subject, consider approaching different people for feedback. For example, my book, *Fundraising for a Community Project* (How To Books, ISBN: 9781845281748), gives advice to small community groups about how to look for grants and apply for grant funding. This is something that I used to do as part of my job before I became a full-time writer. Prior to sending the final draft to the publisher, I asked two people to read it through for me. One was someone I used to work with who checked that my advice was still correct! That sorted out the technical aspect, but I also wanted to know if my text was practical enough for my target reader. So, I asked a friend who I knew was involved with a community group and who had some grant experience. She was able to give me feedback about whether the language I had used was appropriate for my intended readers. I was then able to revise the book taking their comments into consideration. As a result, I was much more confident in the final text when I was ready to submit it to the publisher.

The positive feedback I have since received from readers of *Fundraising for a Community Project* also demonstrates that getting this constructive criticism was the right thing to do. They've benefitted from the steps I took to ensure that they would under-stand what it was I wanted to say.

Start Your Next Project Immediately

Another important technique for dealing with rejection is having more than one piece of work submitted at any one time. It is imperative that as soon as you send something off, you start work on your next idea. NEVER walk back home from the post box and sit and wait for the postman to deliver the reply.

Firstly, you don't know how long the wait will be! I've submitted articles to magazines and not heard anything from them for over five years. That's a long time to hang around!

Secondly, if all your dreams and aspirations rest on one piece of writing, you are setting yourself up for a major confidence crushing moment, should the piece be rejected. And as I've pointed out earlier, a rejection may be for any number of reasons.

However, if, in the meantime, you've written and submitted five other pieces of work and that first piece comes back rejected, all of your dreams and hopes do not rest with that first piece. Okay, so the first piece wasn't accepted, but any of the five others you've written since then and submitted could be accepted. **THERE IS STILL HOPE**. It's still possible to believe in yourself as a writer, because after all, you've written five more pieces since you submitted that first piece. That is something to be proud of.

Talk to other jobbing writers about how many short stories or other items of work they have out there at any one time and many will give you a number ranging from between 20 and 50, if not higher. Writing is a habit that you acquire by repetition and the more pieces of work you have submitted, the greater the chances of success. The more you practise a task, the better skilled you become, which in itself will increase your chances of success.

The more writing you do, the more of it you have to send out there into the big wide world.

Remember the proverb

'Never have all of your eggs in one basket.'
Invest your writing life in lots of different writing projects.

Booster Cards

I've shown you that rejection WILL happen and that on most occasions it probably isn't down to your writing skills. So, how else can you keep yourself going when work is rejected? In my opinion, everyone should have a BOOSTER CARD. As your writing career progresses, this one card will grow into several. But what exactly is a booster card? It's another tool in the psychological battle of remaining positive. It's a way of reaffirming your belief that you are a writer.

My booster cards began life as a small 6 x 4 inch index card. You could just as easily set up a word processing document, but it is helpful if your cards are to hand when your computer isn't switched on, i.e. when the postman delivers the latest round of rejections... I mean fresh learning opportunities... first thing in the morning.

Whenever you feel that 'uh-oh' moment appear at the back of your mind – you know the one, it starts off as a small niggling doubt, which then escalates into a bigger, negative misgiving that eventually tells you to *"give up, you are not a writer,"* – then whip out your booster card and beat those thoughts into oblivion. Read the statements on your booster card and remind yourself that YOU CAN do it. But, what sort of statements should you put on your booster card? Well, positive ones, of course!

Have you won any writing competitions? That makes you an award-winning writer! It doesn't matter whether it was the Booker prize, the Pulitzer Prize, the Commonwealth Writers' Prize or a competition run by your local writers' group. YOU won. YOU pleased the judges with YOUR writing skills. So, put it down on your booster card and write it in CAPITALS. Let it shout YOUR success back at YOU! Go on!

I AM AN AWARD-WINNING WRITER!

Have you had anything published? It doesn't matter whether it was a letter in your local newspaper, a short story in a magazine, or a local historical article in your parish newsletter. Put it down on your card.

I AM A PUBLISHED WRITER!

But I'm not even published yet, I hear you cry! Stop being negative! There are still positive phrases you can put down on your booster card. Are you working on anything now? It doesn't matter what it is, but is there a project that you're tackling at this moment in time. Is it a novel? Is it a poem? Is it a short story? If you can honestly say that you are working on it (and it hasn't been stuck at the bottom of the desk drawer for the last six months) then put it down on your card.

I AM A WRITER! I AM WRITING NOW!

Have you completed an article, short story, or a poem? If so, write it down. Many people start writing projects, but never finish, so completing a piece of writing is an achievement. You can't send off a half completed short story can you? So put it down on your card.

I WRITE COMPLETE ARTICLES / SHORT STORIES / POEMS!

Perhaps you have achieved something big? Have you already written a whole novel? Have you managed to produce something of between 80,000 and 150,000 words? If so, that is FANTASTIC! Yes, that's right. You have achieved something AMAZING! There's a well-known saying that *'Everyone has a book inside them'*.

Indeed, some critics argue that that's where many should stay, but several people do have a go and start writing one anyway. Yet that's all they achieve. They *start* writing it. They never finish it. (But if they've read the section of this book about short, medium and long-term goals then they wouldn't have this problem!) Completing a whole novel is a huge undertaking, whether it achieves publication or not. Be proud of the fact that you can sustain a story for that number of words. I accept that the first novel I wrote is my bottom-drawer novel. It will never see the light of day, nor do I want it to either! Yet it enabled me to prove to myself that I COULD write something of this length and it gave me the confidence to have another go. (Which I did, and the second one was longer.) So, add it to your list and write it down on your card.

I HAVE WRITTEN A COMPLETE NOVEL!

Once you've written something, do you send it off? It doesn't matter whether you submit it for publication or send it to a competition; you are actually doing something positive with your work. Many writers don't send their work out, because they are scared about being rejected. Writers who NEVER send their work out will NEVER be rejected. But then, neither will they be published, nor will they EVER win a writing competition. So put it down on your booster card.

I GET REJECTIONS!

See? I told you every negative has a positive! Getting rejections proves that you're not scared to send out work. You can only be rejected if you've sat down and written something in the first place. Daydreamers don't get rejected. Only *real* writers are rejected. Rejections PROVE that YOU are WRITING and SUBMITTING work. Rejections prove that you are a *real writer*.

Well done you!

> *"The road to success is dotted with many tempting parking places."*
> *Anon*

Keep adding to it

Just like your writing goals, booster cards are not set in stone. In fact, if you practise what I'm preaching in this book, you should find yourself being able to add to your booster cards on a regular basis. If anything positive happens with your writing, then add it to your card.

One such statement I put on my own card was, I HAVE A FASHION COLUMN! (Actually, I had five or six exclamation marks after this one, I couldn't believe it myself.) Now, I openly hold up my hands and declare that I have no fashion sense whatsoever. In my opinion, if it fits, then that's a bonus. But a magazine that I worked for regularly asked me if I could produce a small monthly feature about outdoor clothing. Being freelance, the words, *"Yes, of course,"* uttered from my mouth before I'd even had a chance to think it through properly. I had never dreamt of having a fashion column, nor did I really think that 500 words a month on wax jackets or wellington boots constituted fashion, but I have it in black and white. Those pieces were published in the magazine under the heading *Practical Fashion with Simon Whaley*, which always makes me smile. If I'm writing something and feel as though I am out of my depth, it is *that* statement on my booster card that changes my mindset. If I can carry out whatever research is required to produce a monthly fashion column in a magazine for 12 months, then I know that I can write about practically anything!

When a member at the writers' circle I go to completed her novel, she sent the first three chapters and a synopsis to a publisher. A few months later, the publisher rang up and asked to see the whole manuscript. To say she was ecstatic is an understatement. I told her to write this down on her booster card, because this is an incredible achievement in itself. How many other writers can say this on their booster cards?

PUBLISHERS RING ME UP AND ASK TO SEE MORE OF MY WORK!

Although it doesn't carry the excitement of a definite commitment to publish, it still sends a clear message about her work.

- ☺ She CAN write in an engaging manner.
- ☺ She CAN interest a publisher in her work.
- ☺ She CAN write a synopsis that tells a publisher how her story is told.

All of these are valid statements that she can put on her own booster card. Whenever she has a moment of despair, all she needs to do is read those statements to remind her that she **IS** a success and has already achieved something that many writers dream of.

I mentioned at the start that this book began life as a workshop I gave to the writers' group that I go to. Part of that workshop included creating these booster cards and as we went around the room identifying all of our successes, it was amazing to hear what those achievements were. We had published article writers, poets whose work had been read out on national radio, winners of national competitions and several self-published successes. There were also statements from people who had not achieved publication success, but who'd still had numerous writing successes to claim. Some members had entered every one of the group's own regular monthly writing challenges, whilst others were chuffed at having made the meeting. Yes, tearing yourself away from all of life's other commitments to find two hours on a regular basis to go to a writers' circle meeting is a success in itself.

Everyone listed some successes even though our writing experiences and achievements are different. If there is something to do with your writing that you have achieved, then write it down. It doesn't matter what it is. ALL ACHIEVEMENTS SHOULD BE CELEBRATED.

I began this book by telling you that I've written a bestselling book, am a regularly published writer, and won several prizes along the way. These are just some of the statements that I have on my own personal booster cards. It's a system I continue to use today. Every time I achieve something new, have a success with a new market, or a new writing-related experience (an interview on radio, or an invitation as a guest speaker at a writers' conference), I write it down. It's a good habit to have. It's a positive habit to have.

Make it a Monday morning ritual

As a full-time writer, Monday morning is the start of my working week (and Sunday evening, not Friday, is the end!) Although this is a Monday morning ritual for me, it may not take place on a Monday for you. Nor may it happen for you in the morning either. If you have a set time when you sit down to do some writing, however short this period may be, give yourself a few minutes just to read the statements on your booster cards. Remind yourself of what you have achieved so far and give yourself the psychological boost you need to encourage you to continue pushing forward to achieve your short, medium and long-term goals.

At the start of your writing week, it's all too easy to think of those medium and long-term goals. You might still be hung-over from a particularly good weekend, or know that this week you have a deadline looming. Looking at those medium-term goals may even be off-putting! *What do you mean? This time next week,*

I'll have added another 5,000 words to my novel! Not how I feel at the moment, I won't.

So, collect your booster cards together and read the statements on them. In fact, read them out loud. Forget what you need to achieve by the end of this week, and remind yourself what YOU HAVE achieved so far. Remind yourself that YOU CAN do it. YOU WILL soon learn that whilst this Monday morning feeling is common, it needn't be the controlling factor in the day's activities. You CAN overcome it. Review what you achieved last week and look at your short-term goals for today. That's all you need to focus on. Clear your mind of what you will be doing tomorrow. You will, and can, do that tomorrow.

Achievement Files

Your own personal booster cards are one form of defence against periods of negativity. In addition to your booster cards and when you begin to have any kind of success, you should also set up and keep an achievement file. A ring binder will suffice and perhaps some of those clear plastic wallets to help protect the paperwork too.

This is the place to file all those bigger achievements. Whenever you have anything published, cut it out of the magazine and store it in your achievement file. If you receive a certificate for being Highly Commended in a short story competition, or if you are fortunate enough to be awarded First, Second or Third prize, slip it in your achievement file.

Perhaps you've received an email from an editor at a magazine rejecting your short story but asking to see anything else you might have. If so, print it out and put it in your achievement file. Not every writer gets emails from editors asking to see more work!

An achievement file reinforces your booster card. On those days when I get several rejections, it's easy to slip into a negative mood. Sometimes the statements on my booster card aren't enough to enable me to refocus my mind. My achievement files always do though. This is because the evidence is there in black and white, proving that I CAN do it. I remind myself that I can do it again, because I have done it before. However, unlike my booster cards, which contain my own statements and opinions about my work, my achievement files are what I call *third party boosters*. They are OTHER PEOPLE'S opinions and that's an important difference.

My achievement files contain:

☺ Copies of published articles. This is the evidence proving that other editors have thought my writing is good enough to publish in their magazines. It's also a good idea to keep a copy of everything, so that when you want to pitch an idea to another editor, you can send them a photocopy, proving you are a published writer.

☺ Competition certificates. This means ANY certificate, from the first prizes right down to a commended. I even keep letters from competition organisers who tell me that my short story didn't win, but did make the final shortlist of 25. My story may not have been a winner on this occasion, but somebody else thought it was better than several hundred other entries and that's still an optimistic point to note!

☺ Printouts from websites. If there is an editorial process involved (i.e. it isn't just uploaded on to a website), then I print these out and store copies of them here too. Again, they are just like articles, proof that someone else has thought the work good enough to put on their website.

☺ Letters/emails accepting work. I have all the letters and emails from publishers accepting my book proposals. I even take a photocopy of the advance cheques. Those are really good days and the memories come flooding back whenever I look at them!

☺ I'm fortunate enough to have been on the bestseller lists, so I keep copies of those lists in my achievement files. No one can ever take those achievements away from me.

☺ Letters published in a magazine or newspaper's Letters Page. Whether they are short 15-word statements or 250 word opinion letters, they are still published pieces. Editors still chose my words over those of someone else.

As you can see, your achievement files can contain a varied mixture of evidence of your successes. Keep hold of anything that you have published, whether it appears in your writers' circle anthology, your community newsletter or a national newspaper. And ensure that you continue to add to it. EVERY success has a place in these files. Think of the sense of achievement you will have when that first folder is full and you have to start another one! When you do need to start another folder, make a big thing of it. Go and treat yourself to a nice folder, not an ordinary ring binder. Think of it as another reward for meeting your long-term goals of becoming a more prolific writer.

As your success grows, these achievement files begin to tell your writing story. Flick through your cuttings and printouts and YOU WILL see how you are progressing and developing as a writer.

Your achievement files become your portfolio. Not only are they important for reminding yourself of what you have achieved; they are also great for showing around to friends and relatives. Take them along to your writers' group whenever you have added something new to it. Let other people turn round and say, *"Well done, that's excellent!"*

As writers, it's so easy to hide away in our private garrets and let the paranoia take over. To remain positive and therefore productive, we need to blow our own trumpets. It is often something we're not very good at, but YOU HAVE to do it because when you're shut away on your own in your writing space, nobody else will.

Writing CV

As soon as you see any writing success, create a Writing Curriculum Vitae. Most of us are used to having an employment curriculum vitae, a document listing when we went to school, what grades we achieved in those exams that children never seem to sit these days, and all those other employers whom we've worked for over the years. A writing curriculum vitae ignores all of that stuff. A magazine editor isn't interested if you spent three years working as a traffic warden, unless the article, book or story you are proposing is about being a traffic warden. Instead, your Writing CV only concentrates on your writing achievements and experience.

My Writing CV lists:

- ☺ The books I've had published. I state the year of publication, the title and anything special about them, such as any good sales figures!
- ☺ The publications my articles have appeared in. I don't list all the articles I've had published, I hint at a selection of magazine titles that my articles have appeared in. I also clarify which titles I've regularly written for. It's possible to put a more positive spin on some of the information here. For example, if you've had three pieces published in *Train Spotter's Weekly* and four pieces published in *Pipe Cleaning Today*, you could say that you've had several articles published in *Train Spotter's Weekly* and *Pipe Cleaning Today* magazines. Don't be tempted to embellish too far. If you claim that you've had hundreds of articles published in a magazine, anyone looking at your CV may ask to see the evidence!
- ☺ The publications my short stories have appeared in. Again, I list a selection of the magazines. Include any foreign titles in this list too!
- ☺ Competition wins and placements. Yes, I include seconds, thirds, and highly commended placements as well as the first prizes.
- ☺ Include details of any memberships of any writing related organisations. For example, I mention my membership of the Society of Authors, The Bureau of Freelance Photographers and The Outdoor Writers and Photographers Guild.
- ☺ Any other writing projects. I sometimes work on

commercial projects, such as correspondence courses, or literature for conferences. Do you regularly contribute to your local parish newsletter, or do you write the press releases for your local charity? Mention details of any other writing experience here.

Include your name, address, contact telephone number, email address and a website address if you have one. Then make sure that you update it regularly. Doing this not only reinforces your success, but it produces a document that you can give to anyone, showing your professional career as a writer. And even though you may only be writing for half an hour in the evening, a document like this proves that you take your writing seriously.

Whenever you approach a publisher with a book proposal, or even an editor with an idea for a magazine article, including your writing CV will show them that they are dealing with a real writer. It's a business tool and one that can help bring more work your way, which is just the sort of positive outcome we're looking for!

Brainwashing

To remain upbeat, we need to brainwash ourselves on a regular basis. Don't worry; I'm not intent on establishing a new cult here! (Well, only a positively productive writer one, perhaps!) However, I do hope that by following a few steps in this book you will certainly train yourself to achieve more of YOUR own goals. Cognitive Behaviour Therapy (CBT) and Neuro-linguistic Programming (NLP) look at how a change in the way we think can affect a change in our behaviour. Effectively, this is what being a positively productive writer is all about. Changing our thoughts into positive ones to enable us to change our writing behaviour. Now, I am not professionally trained in either of these areas. The techniques that I describe in this book are techniques and skills that I have discovered and put into practise myself, during my writing career to date. But if this is an area you wish to investigate further, you will find plenty of material about both terms on the bookshelves in shops and libraries, as well as on the Internet.

As far as brainwashing is concerned in this book, it's all about washing the clutter of day-to-day living out of your head, to enable you to concentrate on your writing. Whether you've had the kids screaming at you incessantly all day, had a really big argument with your boss at work, or a run-in with the senior checkout supervisor whilst doing the weekly shop, we need to learn how to wash out that negativity from of our minds. One of the best ways to do this is to pour the brainwashing solution into our heads, through our ears. This is brainwashing through sound.

☺ **Music** Find some music that is suitable to counteract the type of mood you are in. A study by the American Society of Hypertension discovered that people who listened to 30 minutes of classical, Celtic or raga music every day for four weeks had significantly lower blood pressure. Music is calming! So, do you have a favourite piece that you listen to time and time again? Classical music may be calming and soothing and just the remedy after spending the day battling with the outside world. Conversely, if you're preparing yourself to write a highly charged scene between two of your main characters, you may want to listen to something more stirring – *Tchaikovsky's 1812 Overture* perhaps! I enjoy listening to *Enya*, whose music has a soft, Celtic but haunting quality to it at times. It is great background music and I often have it playing quietly, whilst writing. The chorus of her song *Only If* is particularly inspiring. Download the song on to your MP3 player or search the Internet for the chorus lyrics and you'll see what I mean. We all have our own personal tastes in music, so make it a goal to experiment with different types of sound to see which has a more beneficial effect on your writing. You could then write about the results! Create a library of music to help inspire your writing. Again, go back to your own reward system. The next time you sell a piece of work or win a competition, use the money to reward yourself with an MP3 player. It needn't be an expensive one. Use the earphones to block out any distracting sounds and play your inspirational music whilst you're being creative with words.

☺ **Relaxation CDs** Relaxation CDs can transport you to a world away from the stresses and strains of everyday living. They can therefore be a useful tool in your writing regime. I have one to help me escape from those tense, unproductive moments. One of my writing students, Heather Bestel, was a stress management consultant and after the birth of her daughter decided to take her own advice and escape the rat race for a better work/life balance. Her excellent website, www.alittlebitofmetime .com provides some useful advice, as well as her *Just Ten Minutes* and *The Power of Calm* audio CD or MP3 downloads, which are great value. If you're limited to just 30 minutes of writing time a day, it is far better to spend ten minutes listening to a de-stressing soundtrack, enabling you to do 20 minutes of work, rather than waste the full 30 minutes trying to calm down in the first place!

☺ **Inspirational CDs** There are several books and audio guides on inspirational techniques. *Paul McKenna's Instant Confidence* book (ISBN: 978 0593055359) comes with a confidence boosting CD, which you can listen to regularly to help keep your mind focussed on your goals. Whenever you're next in a bookstore or surfing a book website, browse the *Mind, Body & Spirit* section. Don't be afraid to try something new. In fact, make it a reward for meeting one of your short-term goals. Then, this will become a positive action in itself!

Luck

Do you think that some people are luckier than others? I do. However, in my opinion, it has nothing to do with a guardian angel looking over their shoulder and favouring them instead of somebody else. It's all down to you making the most of any opportunity. Those *lucky* people are the ones who work hard at the opportunities that come their way. YOU create YOUR own lucky opportunities.

Was I lucky having a bestseller for my first book? You bet! But it wasn't luck that made me write the book. It was hard work and determination. It wasn't luck that saw four other publishers reject it. It wasn't luck that rewrote the text five times – it was me! Only by putting in the work and effort to write the book in the first place and then learning from my mistakes (the four publishers who rejected it) did I create an opportunity for my book to succeed. Those first four publishers were not appropriately targeted. They were not the right publishers for my material. That was my fault. That wasn't bad luck; that was bad judgement. Only when I realised that I needed to target my manuscript at an appropriate publisher did things begin to go right. Now, I'm not saying that if you target the right publisher, you will have a bestseller. But if you work hard and finish your book and then target the right publisher, your chances of getting it published in the first place are much greater. And only published books can become bestsellers. Half-completed books hiding at the back of desk drawers don't.

When I was signing copies of my book, *100 Ways For A Dog To Train Its Human* (Hodder & Stoughton, ISBN: 9780340862360), at my local bookshop, the owner suggested that I should write one about chickens. In her opinion, chickens were the next big thing. Now, I know absolutely nothing about chickens, but I knew a friend at my writers' circle who did. Diane Perry keeps her own chickens. So I suggested that she have a go at writing *100 Ways For A Chicken To Train Its Human,* using my book as a template. It worked. Her book was published. So was she lucky?

The day you decide to do it, is your lucky day.
Japanese proverb

You could argue that she was lucky that we both went to the same writers' circle and I was able to pass on the idea to her. You could argue that she was lucky my local bookshop owner made the comment about chickens to me in the first place. You could argue that Diane was lucky because she kept chickens and therefore had them to draw upon for her inspiration. Yet when I'd told her about the idea, she could just have easily turned around and said that it didn't interest her. All those *lucky* events had happened *before* Diane decided to sit down and write the book. But they were only *lucky* for her because she then put in the effort. She physically sat down to create 100 separate ideas and then she wrote the book. (And believe me when I say that coming up with 100 different ideas is hard. It is! Try it.) Diane saw the opportunity that existed and grasped it with both hands. She enabled the luck to continue by working hard and making the most of the opportunity that had presented itself. And SHE reaped the rewards.

So, a positively productive writer is one who makes the most of any opportunity that comes their way. They appreciate that they have to generate their own luck. This is a good example of when it is right to be flexible with some of your goals in order to maximise an opportunity. At the time, Diane was working on a children's novel, which she put on hold in order to write this book.

Generally, it is not until I write a speculative piece of writing and send it off that an editor even knows that I exist. Editors who I've never worked with before, or pitched an idea to, rarely ring up with commissions. Those editors who I have written speculatively for on numerous occasions have. I like those days because I feel lucky, yet it was me who created that luck originally by sitting down at my desk every morning and writing that very first speculative piece.

"I'm a great believer in luck, and I find the harder I work, the more I have of it."
Thomas Jefferson

"Luck is what happens when preparation meets opportunity."
Seneca, Roman Philosopher

"I've been lucky. I'll be lucky again."
Bette Davis

Motivation

If ever you find yourself struggling with a particularly difficult piece of writing, it's easy to throw down your pen or push away the keyboard and say, *"Why do I bother?"*

Should this happen to you, then stop what you are doing and answer that very question! Go on. Why *do* you bother? Pick up that pen again, or start a new document on the word processor and write down the answer. Why do you bother writing?

Many writers I know say that they *have* to write. There is something inside us that forces us to sit down and write something. Perhaps its sheer pig-headedness that makes us think we are worth listening to. Sometimes it's because our brains are full of ideas and we have to get them down on paper. Some writers may be looking for fame and fortune, although fortune tends to favour the few! Others just want to see their name in print.

Being a writer means making sacrifices. If your evenings are the only time you have available to write, then you'll have to sacrifice going out in the evenings, in order to get some writing done. Don't become a hermit – you still need to socialise at times, but to do some writing you'll have to sacrifice some evenings' entertainment. That's a conscious decision you are making to your writing. There has to be a good reason for doing this.

If you've identified what your short, medium and long-term writing goals are, then you already have most of your reasons written down. These are what should be motivating you.

Visualisation

One of the key techniques in trying to motivate yourself is visualisation. Writers are good at doing this; we have great imaginations! If ever you get stuck, try to visualise your project, however big or small it is, completed. So if you're writing a novel, try to picture where it will be on the shelf in your local bookshop. Close your eyes and:

- ☺ Picture yourself walking into the bookshop.
- ☺ Imagine looking through your own eyes as you wander through the bookstore to the relevant bookshelf.
- ☺ See your arm stretch out, point your index finger, and then run it along all the spines of the books on this shelf, until you come across your novel.
- ☺ Stop. Pull YOUR novel off the bookshelf and admire the front cover.
- ☺ Picture YOUR name on the front cover.
- ☺ Imagine how you would feel, seeing YOUR name on YOUR book in YOUR local bookstore.

Visualisation techniques can be immensely powerful. One writer I know imagines seeing her article title on the front cover of a magazine, shouting out at passing readers, encouraging them to pick up a copy. It can happen, so why not try it? What do you have to lose?

What this exercise does is reassert in your own mind that you believe in yourself. You CAN do this, if you persist. So, try to combine the visualisation technique with anything on your list of what motivates you to write. This can include:

- ✓ Imagining yourself at an award ceremony, collecting the first prize in a major competition.
- ✓ Picturing yourself at your favourite literary festival with a long queue of people waiting to get your book signed.
- ✓ Seeing yourself turn over a page in a magazine and seeing your letter in print, as the Star Letter.
- ✓ Imagine yourself standing at the back of the auditorium, with every seat in the theatre packed as they all stand to applaud at the end of your play.

✓ Picturing your own short story appearing in a national magazine.

Whatever your dream is, never lose the visual image of that dream. Always picture the moment you are aspiring to. If you find a picture in a magazine or newspaper that encapsulates your writing goal, then stick it up above your computer, or somewhere where you will see it regularly. We need those visual reminders.

Use anything that helps you picture a happy writing moment. If you've won first prize in a competition, frame the certificate and proudly hang it on the wall. Buy two copies of the first magazine you're published in and cut out your piece from one, frame it and hang it up. These visual reminders are the motivating tools to remind you of what you have achieved and what you can achieve again.

When I left my day job to become a full-time writer, unbeknown to me, my friends and colleagues liaised with my publishers to get a copy of the image used for the front cover of my book, *100 Ways For A Dog To Train Its Human*. They had it professionally printed, mounted and framed, then wrote a special message on the back of it, before giving it to me at my leaving party. It hangs above my computer monitor as a reminder of what that book enabled me to do and it continues to motivate me today. Whilst I miss the daily banter of my old work colleagues (daily emails are not quite the same!), that framed image represents to me the moment I gave up the nine to five life of employment and struck out on my own as freelance writer. I enjoy my freelance life far too much to ever want to go back. Whenever I hit a difficult patch, I look up at that picture and suddenly I'm motivated to get going again!

Part III

Putting It Into Practise

Finding The Time To Write

As a full-time, freelance writer, I've discovered that I still don't have enough hours in the day to write everything that I want to write. I began writing for publication at the age of 14. When my first book hit the bestseller lists, my work colleagues often referred to my *overnight success*. At the time, I was 32 years old. In my eyes, my overnight success had taken some 18 years. During that period, I'd tackled my O and A level school exams, spent long hours working for a high street bank and latterly a local government authority. Despite holding down full-time jobs, often working overtime and unsociable hours, I still managed to find time to write. It wasn't easy though.

My first published piece was a Word Search for one of the puzzle magazines. Then I sold an article, and then another and another. By finding the time to write whilst holding down full-time jobs, I had 100 articles published in those 18 years.

Time is a limited resource. It is up to us how we use it. People, who use their time wisely, spend it doing things and activities that are important to THEM.

Yes, it is difficult finding time. There are so many other pressures on this limited resource. Whether it's taking the kids to school, looking after relatives, cutting the grass or doing the weekly shop, there is always something else that needs doing.

The problem with writing is that it is a selfish occupation. It's not a board game that the whole family can take part in after Sunday lunch. It's an individual activity. Admittedly, writing can take place in groups, but only with other writers. These other people know what you are doing and what you are thinking, because they too are doing the same. It's not something that generally works with other non-writers; it only works with like-minded people. As writers, we are selfish people. We crave time to ourselves to enable our brains to go off on an exciting journey somewhere within our own heads. We are only prepared to share this when we are ready and happy with the way our words appear on the page.

The man with the gun

When I ran this as a workshop at my writers' circle, I asked anyone to stick up their hand if they had watched any television at any point during the previous day. Most of them put up their hands. Then I asked them to raise their hands again if they wanted to find more time to write. Everyone put up their hands. Finally, I asked them to raise their hands if there was a masked man holding a gun to their heads, forcing them to watch the television yesterday. Funnily enough, nobody did. Which raised the question, **how much did they REALLY want to find more time to write?** Rarely are we forced to do something we DON'T REALLY WANT TO do.

Subconscious / conscious decisions

What we have to realise is that as human beings, we are continuously making decisions. However, many of these are at a subconscious level. It's not often that we stop and think, *"Right, what shall I do now? Shall I watch television or shall I do some writing?"* After a hard day at work, or battling to put the kids to bed, we often just slump on to the sofa with a drink in hand and stare at the box in the corner with the flashing pictures.

The point I'm making here is that, actually, we do have the time; we just CHOOSE NOT to use it properly. Because you *didn't* have that masked man with the gun to your head forcing you to watch television, it means that you *subconsciously* made the decision to watch the TV. Taking it one step further, it suggests that television was MORE important to you than YOUR writing. But because it was a *subconscious* decision, this thought process doesn't register in our brains and, as a result, we don't take any alternative action.

This is another reason for having a set of short, medium and long-term goals. It will be your short-term goals that will help you turn your subconscious decisions into *conscious* ones. When you've had a hard day at work, eaten an evening meal and put the kids to bed, your short-term goal to write 500 words a day is more likely to be uppermost in your mind (if you haven't already achieved it earlier on in the day). This will lead you to make a CONSCIOUS decision as to what to do next.

Try to make as many of your decisions CONSCIOUS decisions. Stop and question yourself as to why you are doing something. Is it something that you HAVE to be doing now? If not, go and do something else that you HAVE to do. WRITE!

You may decide to sit down in front of the television for half an hour to relax and unwind before starting your writing. This is perfectly acceptable, AS LONG AS YOU DO GET UP AGAIN IN HALF AN HOUR'S TIME AND START SOME WRITING!

In fact, I'm *not* saying that you *must* give up and *can never* watch television again. You could use television as a short-term goal reward. But, what I am saying is, if there's a particular writing project that YOU want to achieve (and remember, it is YOUR writing project, no other idiot is going to write it for you!), is television, or the programme that is on now, *that* important?

For many people, their evening television diet will include one or more of the soaps that grace our screens. One way to find more time to write is to give up watching the soap in the evening. I'm not telling you to give up watching your favourite soap altogether, I'm just saying don't watch it in the evening. Watch the weekly omnibus edition at the weekend instead. (I'll explain more about this later as to why this is a productive idea.) Or, you could simply record it (or use one of the television company's catch-up or on-demand services from their website) and watch it later in the evening as your reward for reaching your daily target.

Other ways to find time to write include:

- ☺ **Early worms and night owls** Which are you? Do you prefer early mornings or late nights? If so, get up half an hour earlier, or go to bed half an hour later. Chances are the rest of the family won't be around then anyway and the house will be quieter. This doesn't work for everyone, but have you tried it? You won't know until you give it a go.

- ☺ **Lunchtime escape** If you find it difficult to write at home, then make the most of your lunchtime at work. If you're lucky enough to have a full hour, give yourself half an hour to get some fresh air outside and stretch your legs, then for the final half hour, find a quiet corner somewhere (or go and sit in your car in the car park) and get out your notebook. If you only have half an hour, make the most of it. Eat your sandwiches and scribble down some ideas. Twenty minutes a day doesn't sound a lot, but it amounts to over an hour and a half in a five-day working week.

- ☺ **Find your library** If you're cooped up at home and can't settle to write there, go out instead. Some people find that, for them, home is not a *working* environment. So, stepping outside of the house and going somewhere else to write can send a strong signal to the brain that you intend to do some work. Go to your local library and work from there. It's quiet, many have coffee shops located inside and any research you need is just a few fingertips away.

- ☺ **Blame the queues at the supermarket!** If you can't snatch some time away from your other half at the library, then can I suggest that you be a bit devious? Most supermarkets these days have coffee shops in them. Whenever you go to do the weekly shop, take your notebook with you. Have half an hour in the coffee shop first. Treat yourself to a nice drink and perhaps even a cake and do some writing in your notebook. (Always write before doing the shopping. If you do it afterwards, you risk your frozen food defrosting!) Then if your other half complains, just blame it on the queues at the till!

☺ **Try telling friends and family.** This works in two ways. Firstly, it sends the clear message that when you are writing you do not want to be disturbed. This doesn't always work though. Family members may still find where you are hiding, barge in and try talking to you. It's just that sometimes they'll say, *"Sorry,"* first, before whining. Secondly, they can be your conscience. If they know that at 8pm you should be going off into the spare room with your notebook or laptop in order to write and at ten past eight you're still slumped across the sofa in front of the television, then they may just provide the disapproving looks and frowns that eventually force you to do so!

The television experiment

A friend of mine, Julie Phillips, undertook a little television experiment. For a week, she aimed to cut down on the amount of television she watched. In fact, she thought she'd try switching it off completely, but with other family members demanding to watch the box, this was a little difficult. Her first 24 hours didn't work out at all! However, she found that if the television was on, she would catch a glimpse of it and be drawn in for a few minutes, before realising that she was failing in her experiment and would then go back to her writing. She realised that a lot of the time, the television was merely background noise.

What's interesting about this is that there are many writers who *need* this background noise. The answer is simple – instead of having the television on with its flashing pictures trying to tempt your eyes away from your writing, all you need to do is switch it off and put the radio on instead. Good background noise, but no distracting pictures.

The next 24 hours were a great success – sort of. Julie managed to avoid the telly all day, but instead of sitting in front of her computer she went manic with the vacuum cleaner and cleaned the house from top to bottom instead!

Day three worked. No telly, no cleaning, just some good old-fashioned writing. At the end of day four, Julie realised that she had completed the first draft of a 1200 word short story from scratch. Success!

Seeing in black and white what she could achieve when she put her mind to it, the rest of the week became easier. When she looked back at the end of the seven-day experiment, Julie saw that her writing output had increased dramatically. Not only had she completed three short stories, but she'd also had numerous ideas for others. In her opinion, her productivity had shot through the roof.

Julie still watches television... but not as much. Now, she uses it as a reward. If she's had a good writing day, she allows herself to watch her favourite programmes, rather than having it switched on all the time and distracting her from what she really wants to do. And since completing her experiment Julie has succeeded in having two of her short stories accepted and several articles published too. The television experiment gave her the time to invest in her writing. Now she believes that she CAN write, so she IS writing, and she is being rewarded by being PUBLISHED.

Undertake a time audit

People often forget that as far as time is concerned, we are all equal. We all have the same 24 hours in a day. Where we differ is what we choose to *do* with that time. For many, there are others who may dictate how much of it is spent. Employers, family commitments and medical appointments decide what we do with our time, but only for parts of the day, not all of it. There are times in the day when we have the power to decide what we do and when. Often, we just don't realise it. Or, to be more accurate, we don't know *when* those times of the day are.

To identify these times, a useful exercise to undertake is a time audit over the period of a week. All you need to do is create a simple table. It doesn't need to be complicated.

Create a grid that has five columns:

- Column 1 is headed up as **Time**.
- Column 2 is headed with **01-15 minutes**.
- Column 3 is headed **16-30 minutes**.
- Column 4 is headed **31-45 minutes**.
- Column 5 is headed **46-00 minutes**.

Underneath these headings, your table should have enough rows to represent each hour of the day you are awake. So, if you get up at 6 o'clock in the morning and go to bed at 11 o'clock at night, you should have 18 rows.

Ideally, you need to do this for each day of the week. There's no need to make this overcomplicated. Simply complete the sheet with details of what you *actually* do with your time during each fifteen-minute block. Every few hours, take a couple of minutes to jot down what you did during those time periods.

Much of that time will be simple to block out; time at work, time spent taking the children to school, time spent doing the family food shopping. But what can be revealing are those fifteen-minute blocks when you don't actually seem to do anything. Perhaps you intended to sit down for half an hour to watch a specific programme on television, and then found that two hours later, you were still in front of the television set. At the end of the day, go through your sheet and pick out any of these wasted blocks of time.

Are there any blocks during your working day that could be

considered useful writing opportunities? These days, the one-hour lunch break seems almost non-existent, but can you get away from your desk for half an hour? If so, why not take yourself off to a quiet corner with your favourite writing magazine? That way, you'll be able to enjoy a writing-related activity whilst also getting an important break from work.

If you can, repeat the time audit exercise and continue until you have a week's worth of data. Then sit down to analyse it. You may find that there are similar times of the day on several days of the week that could be used more effectively. Could you use these times to do a bit of writing? Remember, feeling positive about your writing means getting some writing done. Fifteen minutes here, fifteen minutes there, and another fifteen minutes in the evening doesn't sound a lot, but 45 minutes every day soon mounts up and can lead to some productive writing time! When you know where your writing opportunities are, you can then begin planning when to tackle some of your short-term writing goals.

This audit system can also be a useful exercise to do if you're fortunate enough to have a large block of writing time, say two or three consecutive hours in the day, in which to write. Do you use that writing time efficiently? You may find that breaking that time down into different blocks of activity offers better use of your time. Try spending the first thirty minutes of your writing time catching up on emails and administration, then a further fifteen minutes planning your writing, and then the rest of your time writing. Look out for other opportunities during your day where you may be able to do some different writing-related activities, such as research or background reading, so that these activities don't eat into your actual writing time.

Undertaking a time audit like this not only helps you to identify time when you *could* be writing, but it may also help you to make more *efficient* use of your existing writing time. You'll begin to notice your productivity increasing and this will help to boost your overall positivity.

How many days does it take to create a habit?

Being the creatures of habit that we are, some of the techniques I discuss in this book become really productive when you do them out of habit. Thirty minutes on one day does not achieve much, however, 30 minutes a day, every day for 12 months does. But how long does it take for something to become a habit?

Studies vary, with some suggesting it can happen within 18 days, others quote 21, 29 or even 30 days. I haven't found anything longer than 30 days though. So, as you read through this book, start thinking about how productive you could be in a month's time. That's all it takes. One month (but it could be less). One month to change your life to start achieving what YOU want to achieve.

Sending signals to all and sundry

Making a conscious decision to go off and write not only tells your own brain that you're going to tackle some work, but it also sends the signal to everyone else in the house. It might not always work (there are some people whom you could slap across the face with a sledgehammer and still they wouldn't twig that you weren't happy with them), but if you regularly go off to do some writing, the message will slowly get through. Remember, this isn't just about creating a habit for you, it also means creating new habits for your family to get used to. (*Hmmm, I feel another book coming on: 100 Ways For A Writer To Train Their Family.*) You may still hear the occasional *"Where's Mum?"* or, *"Dad, are you in there?"* although eventually, people will learn.

You MUST be disciplined though. If you tell everyone that you are not to be disturbed for the next 30 minutes and then your partner walks in and asks you to take the dog for a walk, you have to ask whether it is urgent. Can it not wait until your 30 minutes is up? If *you* agree to walk the dog, what have *you* achieved? It is YOU who has sent the psychological message that it's okay for your partner to interrupt you during YOUR writing time. YOU taught them that. You have demonstrated that YOU don't value YOUR writing time.

All too often, what many people think is urgent or important *can* be left until your writing time is over. Nine times out of ten, nobody will die if things wait another twenty minutes. I know it's not easy; I've had to do it myself. Neighbours now understand that I may not answer the front door even if my car is parked outside, suggesting that I'm home. I don't doubt that I get called an unsociable @!?#*'d behind my back because of it, but I am a writer and I will be writing and that's why I get published. It's not easy telling loved ones to go away, but it comes down to the basic fact that if YOU want to achieve YOUR goals then it *has* to be done at some point. I'm not telling you to ignore family and friends forever – just for the time you have set aside for your writing.

So, tell everyone that between 8pm and 8.30pm, for example, you are not available. Make it known that you don't answer the phone or the door between those times. You may think that some of them are testing you out, when they specifically ring at 8.10pm, or knock on your door, but in all honesty, many will simply have forgotten your proud statements. The resulting action then becomes *your* responsibility. Resolve not to answer the call for attention. There is no law that says you *have* to answer a ringing telephone, or answer a call at the door. YOU need to remain in control and make the most of YOUR time. Eventually the phone calls will stop. True friends will recognise your requests and accept them. The next time you meet up, they may even ask how things are going.

Which means that sending this signal to everyone else also sends an important message to yourself. How will you answer the friend who rings up at 8.45pm and asks how your writing went? What will you say to family members sitting downstairs in the lounge when you re-enter the family unit? Telling friends and family about your regular writing time not only sends an important signal to them, but it also sends a signal to you too. And one that should make you feel guilty if you don't actually do any writing during that time!

Brain Training

Our brains are just like any other muscle in our bodies. They can be trained to perform better. Forget you are a writer for a few minutes and imagine yourself as an athlete. Athletes train their bodies to perform for when they need them to. They undertake warm-up exercises and stretches to coax their muscles into performing at their best. The same goes for our brains too. Most human beings are habit forming. We like the regularity of a routine. As a species we learn by repeating tasks until they become second nature.

Repetition develops into skill.

We learn how to use a new computer programme by using it frequently. We learn what our word processing keyboard shortcuts are by using them time and time again. Writing is just another such skill that we learn by doing it repeatedly. People often say that if you do a task enough times, you can do it with your eyes closed. Becoming a positively productive writer means making the writing side of your life a routine. Aim for the day when you can do it with your eyes closed! (Although, as someone who has never learnt to touch-type, that would be a disaster for me!)

Every time I sit down at my desk each morning, my brain knows that it is time to perform. It is time to start work. It has become a habit. As a result, it is now something I find easier to do. Learn how to train your brain.

Wash away the soaps

I mentioned earlier that it is much better for you to ditch watching your favourite soap during the evening and spend the time writing instead. Catch up with the omnibus edition at the weekend, or online when you've achieved your writing goals for the day. But what's the problem with watching the soap during the week? Why not write at the weekend during the longer omnibus edition? Surely having one longer period of time will mean that there's more chance of completing an article or short story in one sitting? The problem with this mindset is that you end up trying to complete a MEDIUM-TERM goal in a SHORT-TERM time period. When you haven't written for several days, writing a whole piece of work in one sitting will be difficult. You will experience several stops and starts. To remain positive, it is better to write in short bursts. Take lots of small, regular steps along your journey of a thousand miles. Don't save it up for a weekend hike.

It's all because of the regularity. Writing for half an hour for four or five nights out of seven is an easier routine to slip into than writing for two hours once a week at the weekends. There are usually several other things we could be doing at the weekends instead. For some people, there are fewer calls upon their time during the evenings. Sitting down to do something on an almost daily basis (and if you can make it a daily routine, so much the better) trains the brain more quickly to slip into *writing mode*.

Just imagine for example, that you have an idea on a Monday evening. If you've decided that you can only do some writing at the weekends, you have four whole days to get through before you will have any chance to develop the idea further on paper. (And that's assuming that nothing crops up during the week that requires your attention at the weekend instead of your writing.) However, if you wrote for half an hour every evening, you could begin developing the idea on that same day.

Having short-term goals should also help you to write on a daily basis. Going back to the novel writing idea, if you can find time to write every day, you know you need to write 274 words every day to reach your 100,000-word target in a year. If you could only write once a week on a Sunday, your short-term target now stands at 1918 words. Which is an easier short-term target to try to achieve? Fewer than 300 words? Or just under 2,000 words?

Create a Time Standing Order

I used to work for a well-known high street bank and I was encouraged to get customers to set up a regular standing order, transferring some money from their current account into their savings account. For some customers, £50 per month didn't sound much, but over the year, their savings account would be £600 better off, plus interest, without much effort on their part at all. The beauty with small and frequent deposits is that they grow into big and worthwhile sums.

So think of your 30 minutes a day as a Time Standing Order. You might not think that you've achieved much writing at the end of your 30 minutes, but after a year, your Time Standing Order will have produced 182 ½ hours of writing time for you. That's a lot of words.

Remember, you are trying to train your brain here. If you're only able to write once a week, your brain is not going to have remembered what you wrote the last time you sat down. You've slept seven times since then (possibly more!), had more arguments with the kids than you care to remember and coped with numerous other family catastrophes in the meantime. So you're going to have to spend the first twenty minutes or so re-reading what you wrote last time, in order to jog your memory.

Whereas if you write on a daily basis, your memory is more likely to recall what you wrote yesterday, where you are up to in your writing and what it is you plan to write about today. You can still re-read what you wrote yesterday, but you only need to re-read a few hundred words, not a few thousand. Tackling your writing on a daily basis knocks everything else down into smaller, manageable chunks too. It's the best way to train your brain into becoming an optimistically creative muscle.

Steal back time

Is time stolen from you? Do you plan to sit down and do some writing, only to have the school ring up to say that little Tommy isn't feeling well and can you go and collect him? Perhaps you were going to do some writing during your lunchtime, but the boss has scheduled an executive lunch instead? If this happens, it's up to you to steal some time back. Time is a limited resource, so we should be making important decisions about how we spend it, all of the time. Don't do anything that will lead to regrets. Make time for *your* dreams and let it help you to achieve them.

Buy time back if you can afford it. Get a babysitter in for a couple of nights a week. Buy a dishwasher, or get the other half to do the washing up, whilst you write. Use YOUR time to bargain with someone else to get some time back. If you promise to fix the leaky tap in the bathroom, can your other half take the kids or the dog out for an hour? Could your neighbour babysit the children for a couple of hours in return for you taking and collecting theirs from school a few days a week? Get bartering! What is YOUR time worth to YOU?

Writer's Block Doesn't Exist

Ouch! Did that hurt? Good, it was meant to. If you think that you can swan around the house in your dressing gown and slippers just waiting for the muse to strike, then you will NEVER be a productive writer. You can't hang around waiting for the muse to find you, YOU have to get off YOUR backside and go looking for it instead.

When was the last time you bought your favourite magazine and opened it up to find it full of blank pages, with a small apology from the editor saying, *"Sorry, but all our staff had writer's block today"?* See what I mean? It just doesn't happen. Newspapers and magazines all need words and they need them on a frequent basis. Their writers can't afford the luxury of writer's block. And that's exactly what it is. WRITER'S BLOCK IS A **LUXURY**.

As a full-time writer, I don't have time for writer's block. Writer's block doesn't put food on the table. Finished articles, short stories and books do. If an editor rings me up with a job and a deadline, I can't say, *"Sorry, I'm suffering from writer's block at the moment, I won't know what to write."* I HAVE to do it.

In my opinion, writer's block is not an illness, or an affliction, but a state of mind. A NEGATIVE state of mind. If you think you are suffering from writer's block, then try to change your mindset. That's what professional writers do. It is all too easy to sit at our desks, staring at a blank page, or monitor, and panicking because we know we should be writing something, but can't think what to write. Panic is not a creative emotion! Of course, if you've broken your writing dreams down in short, medium and long-term goals, then you should know what your immediate short-term goal is when you next sit down at your writing desk.

Left or right?

Our brains are split into two halves or hemispheres. The right side of the brain controls the left side of our body, whilst the left hemisphere controls the right side of our body. However, back in the late 1960s, an American psycho-biologist, Dr RW Sperry, discovered that each hemisphere of the brain has different ways of working. At a very basic level, his studies suggested that the right hemisphere of the brain undertakes creative thinking, whereas the left hemisphere carries out the more logical thinking.

The creative right side of our brain is more spontaneous. It looks at the bigger picture first and this is where our ideas come from. The analytical left hemisphere likes to look at things in detail, rationally, and then sort things out into order.

It seems to me that writer's block is when the right side of our brain thinks of an idea and then the left side of the brain immediately analyses it and says, *"Don't be so pathetic. That's a naff idea!"* And so you dismiss it and sit there in silence waiting for the right hemisphere to come up with a better idea that the left side will think more highly of. To avoid falling into this trap, you need to stimulate the creative right side of your brain and learn to ignore the analytical left.

Calling all egg whisks

A good right-brain stimulating exercise involves an egg whisk. Actually, it doesn't have to be an egg whisk; it can be ANY ordinary, mundane, boring object. If I'm at a writers' group, I pass it around and ask participants to tell me what the object is that they are holding in their hands. It can be anything they like, EXCEPT an egg whisk. Why? Because an egg whisk is what the analytical, logical thinking left side of your brain is telling you it is!

Adults often find these exercises silly and difficult. As we grow up, we become more aware of our surroundings. We worry about what other people around us think, and become conditioned into saying what we think we ought to say. As a result, our analytical left side of the brain begins to dominate. People often say that as we grow older our imaginations are not as good as they were when we were children. I don't believe that at all. As we grow older, we become more concerned about what other people may think of our ideas, so we stifle them to conform to what we perceive is normal, acceptable, or what is expected of us.

Having an idea means taking a risk and running with it. If it's an idea for a short story, we don't know whether the idea really works until we've finished writing it. That's when we know that it works for *us* as a story, but until that short story is published or is placed in a competition we don't know if it works for anyone else. But it will never get that opportunity unless we develop it in the first place. Have confidence in your ideas, be positive about them and they can flourish. The more ideas you have, the more choice you'll have of which ones to work with. You can then go for the ones that you believe are the strongest, which will give you further confidence in them. So, let's look at some right side brain stimulating techniques.

Techniques to overcome left-brain dominance

☺ Take an egg whisk. Actually, don't. Find something else boring and mundane instead. A paperclip. A ruler. A hosepipe. A paper shredder. A mug tree. An iron. A piece of paper. Anything. Now let your imagination run wild. What else could this object be? Could it be a secret transmitter? What about a rope to lead your main character down into the huge abyss? What if your paper shredder became a writer's block shredder? Set yourself a goal. Try to come up with ten different ideas in two minutes. When your time is up, look at what you have come up with. Can you link your ideas together to form a story?

☺ Open a newspaper randomly and focus on a picture of a

person. Don't read the story, but use the picture to create a character. Where do they live? What is their job? What family do they have? What problems do they have? Now close the paper and open it up again randomly. Pick another person and do the same. Now create a link between these two characters that you have produced. Do they love each other? Do they hate each other? You may be surprised where this exercise takes you.

☺ Learn to understand that your left-brain wants you to think logically. So, if you finished writing a section of your novel yesterday, your left-brain will tell you that the logical place to continue writing is from where you left off. That's the most sensible place to start. Every writer knows that any story, article, novel, screenplay, radio play, etc. has to have a beginning and a middle and an end, but there is no law that says you have to write it in that order! Is there another scene later on that you know you can write? If so, write it now. You can always fill in the gaps later.

☺ Left-brain thinking also likes everything to be neat, tidy, and in order. It encourages us to think that what we write should be perfect, first time around. That's rubbish. Rarely are the first words we write the final, highly-polished ones that we want! Our best writing takes place when we edit. So banish thoughts of perfection. Give yourself permission to write complete drivel. It is better to write complete dross than to write nothing at all. After all, you can edit complete drivel. You can't edit a blank page. The logical left-brain is the perfect companion to have when you're at the editing stage in your writing. This is when you *should* listen to its thoughts and questions. Every writer needs to use both their left and right-brains at some point during their writing. But without the initial right-brain activity, there is nothing for the left-brain to edit!

☺ Try planning your writing in advance. Produce an outline.

A list of bullet points may be sufficient, detailing all of the important things that you want to say. Whether it is an article, or a short story, or the grand novel, planning the structure and knowing which information comes next will help to banish difficult starting moments. Some people feel blocked because they don't know what to write, or what to say. If you have a plan, you WILL know what to say next.

☺ As a full-time writer, another technique I've found useful is to create a list of actions at the end of the day detailing all the things I need to do tomorrow. Effectively, what I'm doing is reminding myself of what tomorrow's short-term goals are. When I sit down at my desk the following morning, that list of actions is staring straight at me and enables me to slip into work mode quickly. I create my list in such a way that two of the items are quickly achievable. I tackle these first. These *quick wins* help to boost the brain and keep me in a positive mood.

☺ Stop in mid-sentence. I've used this trick several times and have found that it works for me. It doesn't work for everyone, but try it to see how you get on with it. When your allotted writing time is coming to an end, slow down and stop writing, but don't complete the sentence. Tomorrow, when you come to re-read the last few paragraphs, you can finish that sentence. It's surprising how often finishing this sentence is enough to get you writing the next. And the next.

☺ Have more than one project on the go. This is what I enjoy about freelance writing. I can be working on a novel, a short story, a correspondence course, an article, a non-fiction book and even a letter for a magazine's letters page, all at the same time. If I find it difficult to get going on one project, I often switch to another. Whether you have 30 minutes or 7 hours and 30 minutes to do your writing, it's important to use that time *writing*. The more projects you have on the go, the easier you will find it to write something on one of them.

☺ Write every day. This is one of the best ways to avoid writer's block. Remember, the brain is a muscle that can be trained. Settle down at the same time every day and you WILL find that writing becomes easier over time.

The Write Place

Another positive step that can help you to train your brain into settling down quickly to write is to have your own writing space. Oh, the joys of an oak-panelled study with a green, leather-topped desk perched beside a large window with stunning views that stretch for miles. Yeah right! My reality at the moment is a corner of a bedroom. But it is *my* writing place. Before you begin clearing out the cupboard under the stairs, you need to understand what sort of writer you are. I need peace and quiet. I need to be able to shut the door and to tell everyone else to s*d off. (Despite what you've read in this book so far, I can be quite friendly at times if I want to be!)

There are some writers who need noise. They need to be precariously perched on the corner of the washing machine during a fast spin cycle, with a dozen under-fives using the kitchen table as a pirate ship and a dozen more using the laundry basket as a submarine. Or they need noise of a different kind. Perhaps they prefer the latest pop music blaring out, or the soothing tones of the weather forecast announcer.

Having a regular place to sit down and write reinforces the action, which sends a message to your brain that you're about to commence writing. This may help you to settle into your writing more quickly. As time progresses and you sit down at the same time at the same place in order to write, the words WILL come easier. You will create that habit I spoke of earlier.

I dream of having my own study. I don't have it... yet. Since the age of 14, my writing place has always been the corner of a bedroom. One day, I will have a whole room dedicated to my writing. I do wonder though, after writing in the corner of a bedroom for all of these years, whether that's the only place that will work for me! There's only one way of finding out! (Yes, it's on my list of long-term goals!)

Using the goal and reward system described at the start of this book, I've gradually *improved* my writing place. I used to have a small computer desk with everything crammed on it. When I became a full-time writer, I bought a proper corner unit that was high enough to get my legs under (I'm over six foot tall) without having to be a contortionist. It has filing cabinets built in and space for computer equipment, as well as room to put a notepad and pens, should I prefer to write by hand rather than type.

Six months later, when I'd delivered the second dog book to Hodder & Stoughton, *100 Muddy Paws For Thought* (Hodder & Stoughton, ISBN: 9780340863473), I bought myself a decent chair. The point I want to make here is that I do have a writing space, even though it's not perfect. I haven't waited until I could create the perfect writing space *before* I started doing any writing. I have been writing and using my success so far to gradually improve my writing space.

It's not my dream writing space, nor is it wholly practical. A lot of my filing as well as the materials I use for writing workshops and my stock of published books are stored up in the loft. I regularly have to stop what I'm doing, open the loft hatch, drop down the loft ladder, go up, rummage around for what I'm looking for, then clamber back down again, return the ladder, shut up the loft and then sit back my desk, only to realise I've forgotten something else up there!

Your writing space doesn't need to be perfect right from the start of your writing career. It needs to be the bare minimum to begin with. If you need peace and quiet, then make sure your laptop battery is fully charged and sneak out to the garden shed or the greenhouse for an hour or two. Lie on the guest bed in the spare bedroom with the laptop poised precariously on your knees, if it is the only place where you won't be disturbed. Go and sit in the car, or drive off to a local beauty spot. Your writing office can be anywhere your laptop or pen and paper are.

This is all well and good during the warmer months, but

during winter, the garden shed can be purgatory. Well, one of the best places to go that's warm is your local library. Try it. Take your laptop, or pen and paper and find a quiet corner to huddle in and work. Take a flask with you. Take a packed lunch. Doing this can make you feel more professional because you are leaving the house and going out to work.

As soon as you start seeing some success, whether it's a placement in a short story competition or an article published, family members will then begin to respect you more, as a writer. That's when they may be more willing to give you space at home. Respect has to be earned, so if you want your family to respect you as a writer, you need to demonstrate to them that YOU ARE a writer. This means doing some writing!

Another reason for having your own writing space is because it gives you control. Having control over the smallest of details (which side of your computer monitor you're going to stand your stapler) makes you happier. Knowing where everything is in YOUR personal space means that you are in control. Every time you sit down in this space, in your little domain, you'll be happier and therefore more positive.

Notebooks

As well as having the right place from which to work, you should also treat yourself to the right equipment for writing. One of the main pieces of equipment *every* writer should have is a notebook, whether you write your text out in longhand first and then type it up, or use them for jotting down thoughts and ideas.

At the writers' circle I go to, I'm known for going on about a particular kind of notebook. They're called Moleskine notebooks and they are not cheap (when compared to other notebooks that are available). But, in the words of a television advert for shampoo, writers should consider splashing out on an expensive notebook, *because you're worth it*! Yes, YOU ARE worth it.

I enjoy photography, so that means spending money on photo-graphic equipment. I try to buy the best lenses that I can afford. One of the best ways to improve the chances of getting a sharp picture is to use a tripod. As someone who enjoys walking too, I obviously take my camera with me on my walks, but tripods can be heavy. So, I invested in a carbon fibre tripod – lightweight, but very strong. It wasn't cheap, but because I invested so much money in it, *I make sure that I use it*.

The quality of my pictures has improved and I've sold many more of those taken with a tripod than those taken without. Not only have my pictures accompanied my articles inside the magazines, but some have also been used as front cover images. Having professional equipment has made me think and act more professionally.

Of course, the price paid for a notebook does not improve the quality of the writing or ideas contained within it. But, if you treat yourself to a notebook that you feel is *special* because it has a nicer cover, or is more durable than the flimsy ones you currently use, you *may* be more inclined to use it. So invest in a notebook that you'll *want* to write in. It will encourage you to write something in it regularly. And that's what we're trying to achieve here. A notebook that encourages you to write in it regularly has to be a good thing!

So, what is it about Moleskine notebooks that I like? Firstly, they're available with hardback covers, which means that they are durable. They travel well, and your notebook should travel with you at all times. They come with an elasticated band, which keeps the covers bound together and the pages secure.

Secondly, they come in a variety of sizes. I've used the small pocket ones to record all my walking route descriptions in. They also come in a slightly larger size (not quite A5 size), which I find ideal for jotting ideas, thoughts and first drafts of articles and short stories in.

They also have a wonderful history. Moleskine notebooks were produced in France by bookbinders who supplied local stationers. Writers like Ernest Hemingway and Bruce Chatwin used them. Van Gogh and Picasso used them to for their sketches. In 1986, the last manufacturer of these notebooks shut up shop; but in 1998, a new company began producing them again. So, if they were good enough for those writers and artists, then why shouldn't they be good enough for you? For more information about Moleskine books visit www.moleskine.com or www.simplymoleskine.com. You can find them available in many bookshops and online stores too.

Of course, you don't have to buy a Moleskine notebook, you can buy *any* sort of notebook you like. They just happen to be the notebooks that I prefer using. My point is that you should buy one that feels special to *you*. Buy one that, as soon as you pick it up, you *want* to write in it. Buy one that makes you *feel* like a writer. Buy one that makes you *act* professionally.

Make it one of your goals to find a notebook that you like. Then you can also use it as a reward. Whenever you finish a project, reward yourself by buying another notebook. You DESERVE it!

Generating Ideas

Of course, one of the easiest ways to avoid writer's block and be a highly productive writer is to have plenty of ideas. Ideas are the life-blood of any scribbler. Notebooks are the ideal place to capture them, but where do we find them? To a positively productive writer, ideas are everywhere. The trick is to catch them when you see them and write them down for future use.

This is why a notebook is so important. The best ideas always strike at the worst time. Remember, the actual physical act of writing helps to reinforce the idea in your memory too.

If you don't carry a notebook around, consider yourself a naughty schoolchild! It's lines for you! Write out 100 times:

"I will carry a notebook with me at all times."

The repetitiveness will train your brain into reminding you to carry your notebook with you at all times. You won't regret it!

Of course, it's no good having all of these notebooks and then not writing anything in them. You must make it a habit of writing down your ideas as soon as you think of them. Ideas have a habit of completely disappearing even though you think that you won't have difficulty remembering them.

When you do feel stuck for ideas, go and find somewhere quiet to sit down with a notebook, or two, and spend time reading them. Flick through the pages, stop at random, and read what you have written. Suddenly, your creative right-brain will be buzzing again! Notebooks are our idea archives, a store that you can raid over and over again.

For some writers, particularly those starting out, ideas seem about as common as big lottery winners. You know that there are some out there somewhere, you just don't happen to know any. So, here are a few idea sources to get you started:

Work Experience

All the pundits tell you to write about what you know, so what have you done for a job? I spent six years working in the community grants area for a government department and later a local authority. I used this knowledge to write my book, *Fundraising for a Community Project*. My first job was with a major high street bank and I wrote an article for the Guide Dogs for the Blind Association magazine about the guide dogs we had running around the office! I've also used the experience to co-write *The Bluffer's Guide to Banking* (Oval Books, ISBN: 9781903096529). It doesn't matter what your job is, there are ideas to be found. Do you work in a supermarket? Well, write an article about the best time to buy food at reduced prices. What tips would you offer to those who'd never used Internet shopping for their groceries? Can you set a short story in a super-market? (The answer is yes – I've sold supermarket-based short stories to magazines in the UK and Australia.)

Personal Experience

I've been blown up by the bomb squad, been part of a winning lottery syndicate (see I told you there were winners out there – now you know one – I've spent it by the way so don't bother with the begging letters) and I've been hot air ballooning. I haven't used the first experience yet, although I'm sure I will do. But I have written about the lottery win and the ballooning experience. In fact, whatever you have done, try to dig an idea out of it. Lynne Hackles' book *Writing from Life* (How To Books, ISBN 9781845284190) offers some excellent guidance on doing this.

Remember, the idea for this book came from the workshop I gave at my writers' group. I've written an article about a holiday in West Wales when all it did was rain – and it was published. I used my time between events at a literary festival to write an article about the benefits of going to a literary festival. I do a 45-

minute walk every day and I've written about that in article form (and you'll read more about that a bit later on, too). Whether you're out walking the dog (there's another one – I wrote an article about what clothes to wear when taking the dog out), or shopping at the supermarket and getting the most points on your loyalty card (that was my first published short story) ideas are around everything that you do. Write a list of things you've done today and see what ideas you could generate from them.

Hobbies

What are your other interests, apart from writing? What advice would you give others thinking about taking up the same hobby? How did you start out? What mistakes did you make that they can learn from? I've always enjoyed walking and some of my first published pieces were with the walking magazines. Not only have I regularly contributed walking routes to a walking magazine and a local magazine, but I've also written two books, *Best Walks in the Welsh Borders* (Frances Lincoln, ISBN: 9780711227668) and *The Bluffer's Guide to Hiking* (Oval Books, ISBN: 9781906042073). Writing about your hobby can be a great way to break into print. If the subject matter interests you, then the enthusiasm will show in your writing too. It also makes you a bit of an expert in the subject compared to the average person on the street.

Travel

With the exception of a couple of school trips to France and Germany several years (make that decades) ago, I haven't been any further away from mainland Britain than the Isle of Wight and that's only a five mile boat trip! But I shall never forget the Isle of Wight. It was a nightmare trip and one I've written about on numerous occasions, so it has served me well in my writing! In addition to the many letters to magazines on the subject, I also used the episode for the *My Crap Holiday* section in *The Observer's*

Travel pages. You may still be able to find it online at: www.guardian.co.uk/travel/2008/oct/19/isleofwight-walkingholidays

However, remaining in the UK hasn't stopped me writing numerous travel features. My travel articles have appeared in *Hotel, In Britain, The Lady, Holiday Cottages, British Life, Country Walking, Dogs Monthly* and *The People's Friend* to name a few. Obviously, I've written about British places, but everywhere is a place to visit to somebody. So, look around your own hometown. Where would you advise a tourist to visit? You should know – you live there! That makes you an expert. And just because it might not be on the normal tourist trail, that doesn't mean to say that you can't write about it as a tourist destination. The fact that it isn't in a holiday hot spot may actually be enough to interest an editor. And if you do live in a tourist hotspot, as a local, do you know of places that are not mentioned in the guidebooks? Again, it's your local knowledge that makes you a mini-expert in this subject.

Pets

I have to mention pets. As the bestselling author of *100 Ways For A Dog To Train Its Human* (Hodder & Stoughton, ISBN: 9780340862360) it goes without saying where my inspiration for that particular book came from! One thing I like about ideas is watching them grow and this is one that certainly blossomed. The idea for *100 Ways For A Dog To Train Its Human* originated as a magazine filler. I still have a copy filed in my achievement file. It was 100 words in length and I received £25 for it. But, the idea kept bubbling away and I expanded this into an 800-word article called *How To Be The Perfect Dog Owner*, which was published in *PetDogs Magazine*. Eventually, the idea expanded into the book, which was then followed by a sequel, *100 Muddy Paws For Thought*. If you have a pet, then use that experience. I've written numerous articles for dog magazines about how to find the perfect self-catering holiday cottage for you and your dog, how to avoid the beaches that dogs are banned from, what the right to roam open access countryside agreements in England and Wales meant to dog owners, and so on. Magazines also love funny stories involving our pets, especially if you have pictures to back them up.

Photographs

Talking of pictures, photographs can be a great idea generator. Flick through your holiday snaps and see if they inspire anything. I've used my holiday snaps to create travel articles about the Royal Yacht Britannia, a feature on the city of Chester, and ten top walks in the Lake District National Park accessible by bus.

If you don't have a camera, use other people's pictures to stimulate ideas. Flick through a magazine, focus in on one person and create a story about them. Find an idyllic cottage in one of the self-catering holiday cottage brochures and imagine using it as the setting for a short story.

Eavesdropping

Right, let's get one thing straight. Eavesdropping isn't rude… if you're a writer. In our case, it's RESEARCH. Whenever you hear snippets of information, write them down in your notebook. As I overheard one woman say to her daughter in the upmarket Cotswold village of Stow-on-the-Wold, *"I quite agree with you, darling, it is a lovely car, but she hasn't got the breeding to carry it off has she?"* Priceless! What does that tell you about character? I haven't described the woman at all, but I know that you have an image in your mind now don't you? It could be the start of a short story, a radio play or even a novel. If ever you're worried about being caught eavesdropping, try putting some of those small earphones in your ears and plugging them into an MP3 player or radio, but don't switch it on. That way, everyone will assume that you are quietly listening to music!

As a volunteer driver for my local Good Neighbour scheme, I occasionally give lifts to people who need to go to the local hospital for outpatient appointments. Whilst they go off to the various clinics, I sit down with some work and a cup of tea in the hospital café, where I've overheard many an interesting conversation. On one such occasion, there were two nurses sitting at the table behind me:

"I'm going to have to tell him."
"But why?"
"Because he's got a right to know."
"Can't you keep this to yourself a while longer?"
"I can't keep it quiet forever can I? He's going to notice at some point isn't he? I'm just so scared of how he will react."
"What are you scared about?"
"What am I scared about? What am I scared about? BECAUSE IT'S ORANGE!"

At this point they got up and left. Now, don't tell me that your mind isn't busy coming up with several possible scenarios! But no, I do not know what it was they were talking about!

Recycling

Idea generation is a bit like brain training. The more frequently you do it, the easier it becomes. In the meantime, make the most of any idea you have by recycling it. You'll surprise yourself as to how many more ideas crop up that way. I've written articles about Heritage Coasts. This is a protection status for the English and Welsh coastline, a bit like the Area of Outstanding Natural Beauty or National Park status. I've sold articles about the Heritage Coast status to county magazines in Norfolk, Suffolk, Dorset, Yorkshire, Kent, and Sussex, a magazine covering Wales, and a walking magazine. One basic idea, eight published pieces. I twisted the information in each of the articles to make them fit the local magazines, but my basic research about Heritage Coasts covered me for all of these articles.

When I visited Scotland's capital city, Edinburgh, I went on the Royal Yacht Britannia and fell in love with it. If ever you get a chance to visit it at Leith Docks, then go. From that one trip, I've sold three magazine articles, and one short story.

Every so often in Britain, we have earthquakes that we actually feel. I wrote an article about them for *The Lady* magazine, used most of the information in an article for a Wales magazine about the last big quake to hit the Principality and I've sold an article to magazines in Derbyshire, Cumbria and Yorkshire about their last big quakes. Again, one idea, which has resulted in five published pieces... so far!

The bells! The bells!

Here's an idea that I sometimes use at workshops, which you can adapt for yourself at home. I have some of those hotel-reception-type bells that you 'ding' to call for attention. Whenever I have a group of writers together and I ask them to brainstorm in groups for ideas, I get them to 'ding' the bell every time they have an idea. It usually ends in complete chaos, because there is so much noise! However, to someone like me who is facilitating the workshop it's great because I know that they are coming up with lots of ideas. The noise reinforces the action. It also generates a bit of competition, hence the chaos. In its simplest form, dinging the bell is merely a short-term reward for a short-term goal.

Can you find an alternative reward system for every time you have an idea? There are electronic gadgets you can buy that call out fun phrases, for example. Or perhaps a small monetary reward would work? You could add a coin into a jar every time you have an idea, or put a small coloured sticker on the calendar for today's date. Whatever you do, keep your reward system simple and take pleasure from being able to stop and look at how many ideas you've had recently.

Ten (foot) Steps To Productive Writing

I do a lot of writing with my feet. No, not literally – if I did, I wouldn't be able to read what I'd written! However, I've found that going for a walk can often solve my writing problems. It clears my head. That thinking time, whilst I'm out walking, can be so productive I still call it *writing time* even though I'm not sat at my desk.

Sitting still for long periods is not good for our bodies. Our shoulders curl over our keyboard, bending our spine unnaturally. Chained to a desk all day drinking tea or coffee and grazing on biscuits is not healthy – and remember, the brain where all of our work takes place is still part of that body. Garbage in, garbage out, as they say! Going for a walk helps to stretch those muscles and provides our body with a good workout.

Endorphins

Walking has a beneficial effect on our health. It causes the brain to release endorphins, a chemical that not only acts as a natural painkiller, but also works as a positive stimulant. Some doctors now prescribe walking to patients experiencing mild depression. So, if the words aren't flowing and your writing time feels unproductive, stop what you are doing and go for a walk.

A few years ago whilst on holiday, I was writing a short story and hit a problem. The beginning and the middle were there, but the ending wasn't right. No matter what I did, or thought of, I couldn't create a satisfactory ending. So I got up, put on some shoes and went for a walk.

Within ten minutes, the fresh air and stimulating surroundings had done their work. I suddenly had a solution and busily scribbled it down on my notebook (because I like to have one with me at all times). When I got back to the cottage, I sat down and rewrote my ending. I was happier now. It worked.

Two weeks later, I sold the story to *Take a Break* magazine.

To find solutions to some of your writing problems, try following my next ten footsteps on a path of discovery. The journey will be amazing and will ultimately help you on your long-term journey of a thousand miles.

Footstep 1: Go for a walk everyday. It doesn't have to be miles long; in fact it's probably better if you think in time rather than distance. Can you get to your local park and back in 30 minutes? Why not wander around to your local coffee shop? As the weeks pass by, you'll notice your general fitness levels increase along with your stamina.

Footstep 2: I shouldn't have to say this, but make sure you take a notebook with you. Any solutions that suddenly become apparent can then be quickly jotted down. New ideas often come to me whilst I'm out walking. (I've already told you that I wrote an article on this very topic for a magazine – where do you think that idea came from?)

Footstep 3: Vary your route. Don't do the same route everyday. Try to devise three or four different routes if you can and alternate between them. Variety adds interest and heightens our senses. It makes the brain more alert and you'll notice more of the smaller details, which you can use to make your writing more interesting to readers.

Footstep 4: Vary the time of day that you go out. Go first thing in the morning one day, at the end of the day on another and during your lunch break on the third. Or you could just look out of the window, wait for the rain to clear up and go then. Whatever you do, don't create a regular routine that allows you to do the walk with your eyes closed! That's not what you're trying to achieve.

Footstep 5: When varying your route, try to find something interesting along the way that can stimulate your mind. Find an inspirational view, wander through a churchyard and make up stories about the people you come across (dead or alive). In my local churchyard there is a gravestone to Ann Cook, which says:

On a Thursday she was born,
On a Thursday made a bride,
On a Thursday broke a leg,
And on a Thursday died.

Now there's some inspiration for an article or short story!

If you find graveyards a bit too creepy then stop and read the cards in your local newsagent window or the notices on your community notice board. Is there anything interesting for sale? Perhaps someone is offering some unusual services? Whatever you do, don't pound the streets quickly, in an effort to get back to your desk and back to work. Stop. Take time to absorb your surroundings.

Footstep 6: Take a camera with you. Capture scenes that inspire you. Even if you tackle the same route on a Monday and a Thursday, the chances are you'll be doing them at different times of the day and in different weather. The lighting will be different. You will see something new every time. Train your brain to look for new sights on EVERY walk.

Footstep 7: Leave your mobile phone at home. This is not the time to be contacted. This is time for YOU. This is time for YOUR brain. Go for a walk on your own. Escape from the world and think about the things that are important to you.

Footstep 8: Use your notebook to jot down things you experience. What do you see? What do you hear? How do you feel? Is it a warm day or is it cold? What can you smell? Put all of these experiences down. Why? Because the more of our senses we draw upon, the more we use them in our own writing. One day you'll be flicking through your notebook and suddenly you'll stumble across the perfect description that you've been racking your brain for. This reinforces the reason why writers have notebooks. They are an investment in our future writing.

Footstep 9: When you get back, sit down and read through your notebook. Re-live your walk. Reinforce those ideas that came to you whilst you were out and the chances are they'll spark off new ideas too. Don't forget to write those down.

Footstep 10: Write! Now you're back at your desk, develop those ideas and work on them. Go back and complete the piece that you were working on earlier or start something new that came to you whilst you were out. Learn to accept that you may not find the solution to your writing problem on one walk, but develop those ideas that do come to you. It took three weeks to get a solution to a problem I had with a novel I was writing, but in those three weeks of walks, I had over 20 other ideas.

Learn your Latin: **Solvitur Ambulando**
Which means "You can sort it out by walking."
It's true.

Still not convinced? Let me tell pass on another bit of information then. Research from the University of Illinois suggests that three hours a week of brisk walking can reverse the brain deteriorations brought on by ageing. So, walking not only boosts the brain's grey matter neurons into action, which helps our thinking process, it also reduces the amount of brain shrinkage as we get older. The more walking you do, the more brain matter you'll have to inspire yourself with more ideas! What are you waiting for?

Doing A Fagin

In the words of the immortal song from the musical *Oliver!*, Fagin was always reviewing the situation. So, if it was good enough for him, then it's good enough for me. And it's a great way for you to gain a clearer understanding of how *you* work.

Do you know what it is that makes *you* tick and, more importantly, what helps *you* to create those really good writing periods? When you think about it, we writers are a right bunch of weirdoes really, aren't we? You only have to read those *Day In The Life* articles that appear in the writing magazines to realise that we're obsessed with whether Stephen King has strawberry jam or marmalade on his toast, because it must improve his plotting. And if JK Rowling happens to wear odd socks, then that's the reason for her success and we should all be doing the same. Moreover, does having a desk that faces north-northeast really help the magnetic energy flow through your head, thereby enhancing your creativity?

To write regularly and productively, it's necessary to review our own habits and actions on a regular basis. What those *Day In The Life* columns provide us with is a useful insight into how other writers work. We're all individuals, so what works for some may not work for others, but I've gained many a tip from other writers in these columns. However, before you start copying the great writers of our time, do you know what actually works for *you* and what doesn't? If you can review your own working practises over the period of a week or two, you may be surprised to find out what REALLY works for you. And you'll have a much more positive outlook if you know you're creating the right environment in which to work.

Keep a diary
No, I don't mean a Bridget Jones style diary detailing your

calorie intake and current knickers size, but a *creativity* diary. What do you do during the day and how creative is it? Take five minutes out and look back at yesterday. Did the words flow effortlessly without too much squeezing of blood out of that stone? Did you achieve all of your short-term targets for that day? Make bullet point notes about what you did yesterday and by this I'm not just referring to writing tasks, but *everything*. Did the kids miss the school bus, which meant that you had to take them there in the car? Did the dog chase next-door's cat, causing chaos in the village? Include anything that you ate and drank if it was different from your usual daily routine. What do you think helped to create that frame of mind you experienced yesterday? Did you go to bed early? Did you sleep for eight hours or more? Perhaps it was all down to the Ham and Pineapple pizza you had for tea the night before?

Of course, it works both ways. It should help you to identify moments and activities that led to a less productive day. Was it the 12 bottles of red wine you drank with your friends last night? Or perhaps it was because you went to bed at 9pm instead of your usual 11pm? Whenever you do anything different, make a note and then look back at how it affected your day. Was it for better, or for worse?

At the end of each day, summarise in your diary what type of writing day you had. Now, as positively productive writers, we don't have *bad* days. Bad days are not positive days are they? Instead of recording days as BAD, OKAY or GOOD, I want you to record whether your writing day was GOOD, AMAZING or FAN-BLOOMING-TASTIC!

Reviewing the situation
The longer you can keep this diary going, the better, but don't begin reviewing your habits until you have at least two weeks worth of entries in your diary. Then, take the time to re-read it and pick out any common practises that crop up. Analyse your

FAN-BLOOMING-TASTIC days first of all, before moving on to your AMAZING and then your GOOD days. The information this provides can be very revealing.

I've discovered that I write better if I settle down before midnight the previous night (and manage to sleep through until 6.30am). If I've read a book for pleasure for half an hour before I settle down, the following day is usually more productive because for some reason I sleep better too. A night out generally leads to a poor night's sleep and then a poor productive day after, but I've now learned to juggle my workload so I don't do any creative work on that day. That's the power of a *creativity diary*.

If I have to produce a walk description for one of my regular walking columns, I usually have enough energy left to write the route description when I get back from my trek, but the creative, introductory paragraphs are best left to the following day. I've discovered that the physical tiredness of the day means that I can't produce as good an introduction as I'd like on the same day that I tackle the walk. Yet it was only by keeping such a diary that I spotted this. Before then, I used to get frustrated, because in my opinion the right words wouldn't flow. This frustration would often lead to negative thinking, leading to a further deterioration in my day's productivity. Now, I accept it and know that I won't have a problem tackling these paragraphs first thing the following day. This has enabled me to remain more positive.

Use the information to plan

Once you've collected your data, start to use it to your advantage. I know I'm not particularly creative after a night out. So the following day, I try not to do anything too creative. Instead, I focus on admin, chasing invoices, doing some research, planning articles or sorting out pictures. I don't get anxious now because I'm not being as creative as I think I *ought* to be. And, I know that if I do some reading and settle down by about midnight, I should have a more creative day tomorrow. This takes the pressure off, enabling me to feel more optimistic, which increases the chances of being creative tomorrow.

It also allows me to plan my short and medium-term goals better. If my week includes a day out walking for one of the magazines, then I may lower the daily word count for that day. I usually aim for 1,500 words a day, but a walking route description can vary between 450 and 750 words depending upon the magazine I'm writing it for. As long as I set myself the target of writing and completing the route description on the same day of the walk, I'm happy. And I'm confident that, based upon the information in my time diary, I can produce the balance of the word count the following day, in addition to the following day's word count target too.

However, it is important to be honest with yourself as you analyse your time diary. Are those two hours spent on the Internet doing research really research? Or are you catching up with friends on a social networking site? The Internet and email are huge time gobblers. NEVER set your email programme to collect messages automatically. As soon as a message pops up on your computer screen telling you that you have mail, you will probably stop what you are doing and read it. It breaks your concentration and it reduces your productivity. Instead, collect them manually, by clicking on the 'Send/Receive' button. Every two to three hours is enough. You could make collecting your emails a reward for finishing a short-term goal. If you only have limited time to write during the day, then don't collect any emails during your writing time.

Repeating the exercise

After three months, repeat this diary exercise. Not only is it an opportunity to discover how effective you've now become by putting what you've learnt about your GOOD, AMAZING and FAN-BLOOMING-TASTIC days into practise, but our routines may also change with the seasons. In winter, I tend to do my daily walk just prior to or soon after lunch. Walking around in the dark at 4pm is less inspiring than walking in daylight! However, in the summer I might go for my walk before breakfast, during the day or later in the evening, because it is lighter. Sometimes I find that, during particularly hot periods, I'm more productive working in the early morning and late evening when it's cooler and doing research or reading during the hotter midday time. So take the opportunity to experiment.

When I first began working as a full-time writer, there were occasions when I panicked because I hadn't submitted anything for publication by the end of the day. Naively, this was what my short-term targets were at the time. However, by keeping the diary, I learnt so much about my *creative* self. I know what can lead to a GOOD day and the things I have to do to create a FAN-BLOOMING-TASTIC day. And by understanding how to create a FAN-BLOOMING-TASTIC day, it means that I have learnt how to cope with an ordinary, GOOD day.

Sometimes though, we all need a less productive day just to keep in touch with the rest of the world. Twelve bottles of wine in one night with friends will create a less productive following day (whether you're a writer or not!), but over time it may be just what you need to really improve your productivity. If you average six AMAZING days a week and one FAN-BLOOMING-TASTIC day one week, but a night out with friends generates two GOOD days and four FAN-BLOOMING-TASTIC days, then it's clear to see that the occasional 'dip' in productivity may actually produce a better week overall. As a result, use your time diary to appreciate that your **productivity shouldn't be scrutinised on a day-by-day basis, but assessed over a longer period of time.**

Think back to the goal setting exercise. It is the smaller short-term goals that help us to achieve our big long-term goals. It's the long-term goals that people are proud of and tend to remember, not the short-term goals. Maintaining and reviewing a diary like this helps you to look at the bigger, long-term picture. You may be surprised how much you could benefit from this exercise.

Lists

A friend of mine once described a writer as a Bohemian person who wafted around in a disorganised, spaced-out trance, wearing long, flowing clothes and permanently looking for their reading glasses (which were always on the end of their nose). The reality couldn't be further from the truth (for most writers), but what this suggests is that our creativity is supposedly born out of a state of disorganised chaos. It is not. If you want to be Bohemian, be my guest. Wear the hippy clothes, titivate with your long gemstone necklaces or bracelets and clasp the back of your hand to your forehead as you wander around the house waiting for inspiration to strike you. The female writers amongst you can do the same as well, if you like!

Somehow, I just can't see the journalists of national newspapers doing this. Even novelists have to sit down and write at some point. A deadline is a deadline, whether inspiration has struck or not. It doesn't matter whether you're able to spend all day writing or can only snatch 30 minutes between parental responsibilities; *you* have a deadline too. And when that deadline arrives, you'll have to stop writing and return to your family life. It's therefore imperative that you maximise your writing time and get *organised*.

End of the day

In the section about overcoming writer's block, I mentioned that creating a list at the end of the day might help you to slip into the right frame of mind when you next sit at your desk. So, when your daily writing time is coming to an end, take a minute to jot down what you need to achieve during tomorrow's writing time.

Of course, there is a knack to this. Don't jot down *write*. That's too simplistic! Think back to what I discussed earlier about goal setting. In the same way that your goals need to be S.M.A.R.T.: so too do your lists. That is, after all, what a list is, a series of short-term goals. Here's an example of the list I'd created last night for myself, for when I'd sat back at my desk this morning:

- ☺ Add another 1,500 words to *The Positively Productive Writer*.
- ☺ Liaise with the RSPB about Black Grouse walk re article commission.
- ☺ Chase publisher who's had novel for six months now.
- ☺ Review rejected short story and identify a new suitable market to target.
- ☺ Approach walking magazine editor with article proposal.
- ☺ Write a letter to a magazine letters page.

When creating these lists at the end of the day, write them down as you think of them. Don't worry about the order they appear in. There is no law that says you have to tackle them in that order. However, you should try to include the following in your list:

- ☺ Anything on today's list that you did not achieve.
- ☺ Your normal short-term writing goals.
- ☺ What else you would like to achieve if you can/have time to do so.

On my list above, chasing the publisher and reviewing the short story were items that I'd carried forward from the day before. Adding an extra 1,500 words to this book was my regular short-term goal. Liaising with the RSPB over the commissioned article was a new short-term goal following the magazine's request for me to do the work. Approaching the walking magazine editor with a new idea is part of an ongoing medium-term goal I have of generating future commissions. Writing a letter for a magazine's letters page was an extra item, if I had the time at the end of my day.

Sitting down at my desk this morning, I examined my list and chose to tackle them in the following order:

- ☺ Liaise with RSPB about Black Grouse walk re article commission.
- ☺ Chase publisher who's had novel for six months now.
- ☺ Approach walking magazine editor with article proposal.
- ☺ Add another 1,500 words to *The Positively Productive Writer*.
- ☺ Review rejected short story and identify a new suitable market to target.
- ☺ Write a letter to a magazine letters page.

In the same way that short-term goals help us to feel good psychologically about our longer-term goals, tackling the easier, or quick-win, goals first on the list above helped me to slip into work mode more quickly. With lists, ticking something off is a huge positive boost. In fact, I tend not to tick something off a list, but scribble through the whole text. I literally *obliterate* the list, piece by piece! But again, psychologically, this action helps to keep me in a positive frame of mind as I reduce the amount of work left to tackle. So, dealing with the smaller, easier jobs first helps me to establish this positive frame of mind much earlier in the day.

Liaising with the RSPB meant obtaining some information and arranging a time to meet. This turned out to be a quick five-minute email. Chasing the publisher about the novel they'd been hanging on to for six months took me half an hour (to construct a carefully worded letter, which I hoped would not jeopardise any chances I had!) Approaching the walking magazine editor with a new idea took 15 minutes by email, which meant that in less than an hour I had already crossed off three items on my list. The bulk of my day was taken up with the next item on the list (which was always going to be the case), because it was my main short-term goal that I was aiming for. However, because I'd already tackled those administrative areas of my work first, I found that I managed to settle into the creative aspect of getting on with this book quickly. (Indeed, by lunchtime I had already added nearly 900 words!)

After lunch, finishing the remainder of my word target took me a couple more hours and I spent the rest of my day reviewing that rejected short story. I identified a new target publication to aim for and spent the rest of the afternoon rewriting that short story.

Which comes first? The easy or the difficult tasks?

There is a school of thought that suggests you should tackle the most difficult jobs on your list first. This is because you know your day is going to get easier once they are out of the way. Some people are more switched on first thing in the morning, so tackling the most difficult jobs when their brain is more alert, makes sense. I've found that, for me, tackling the easier jobs first helps me to settle into my day quicker, which enables me to tackle the bigger jobs later on with more ease. There is no right or wrong way. However, for you to be as productive as you can, it is important that you to discover which method suits you best. Try both, and then stick to the one that works for you.

At the end of the day, when I reviewed my list, I discovered that I had crossed everything off, except the write a letter to a magazine letters page. Despite not having achieved everything on my list, I still felt that it had been a great productive day. I had succeeded in getting most of the administrative side of my writing business tackled, as well as achieving my main aim of writing another 1500 words. (It was 1536 actually!) I'd also rewritten a rejected short story for a new market. So, my list for the following day now looked like this:

☺ Add 1,500 words to *The Positively Productive Writer*.
☺ Re-read short story, checking for errors etc, and then print

off submission and post.

☺ Write a letter to a magazine's letters page.

☺ Produce the first draft of my next column piece for The New Writer magazine.

And so it goes on.

Many writers follow a similar system, but they maintain the list in their head. They don't have anything physical to cross off as they go through the day. This can have two consequences. Firstly, they don't actually remember everything on their list. (Remember what I said about jotting ideas down in a notebook? The physical act of writing something down helps you to remember.) Secondly, you can't actually cross something off with a pen in your memory, can you? Having a visual aid at the end of the day showing your achievement reinforces the message again. It's this visual confirmation that helps to keep me in a positive frame of mind and may work for you too.

Which looks better? The following blank space representing the area in your memory where today's list was mentally stored and mentally deleted?

Or, the following visual list, showing what has been achieved because it has been crossed out?

☺ ~~Add another 1,500 words to *The Positively Productive Writer*.~~

☺ ~~Liaise with RSPB about Black Grouse walk re article commission.~~

☺ ~~Chase publisher who's had novel for six months now.~~

☺ ~~Review rejected short story and identify a new suitable~~

~~market to target.~~

☺ ~~Approach walking magazine editor with article proposal.~~

☺ Write a letter to a magazine letters page.

I know which works for me! I find this visual reminder of what has been achieved during the day immensely powerful. So much so, that if I do something that isn't on my list, I will add it to my list and then immediately cross it off, because it is something else that I have achieved today. It may seem strange adding something to a list and crossing it off straight away, but it's part of my psychological battle of staying positive!

Procrastination

I couldn't write a book about being productive and not mention procrastination – the art of doing anything but what you *should* be doing. We all do it, the trick is recognising when we're doing it and then making the effort to start what we should be doing – writing.

If you suddenly find yourself procrastinating, start singing the following words to the tune of Cliff Richard's song *Congratulations*.

Procrastinations, adjournications,
why bother writing when you could be washing up?
Procrastinations, adjournications,
this writing game is not all down to bleeding luck.

When you've embarrassed yourself enough, it's time to start writing!

Actually, the best solution to procrastination is not to embarrass yourself, but to make the task you're putting off easier to tackle in the first place. That's what procrastination is all about. It's a diversionary tactic, busying yourself with some other pointless activity to prevent you from doing what you *ought* be doing, because you think that task will be difficult or complicated.

If you foresee a task coming up that you won't enjoy doing, which may lead you to procrastinate, then it's time to look at that list you've created. Let's imagine that you need to write an article, but this involves ringing up an interviewee and asking them questions to get some good quotes for your piece. Many of my students hate doing this! Again, it's the negativity that takes over, convincing them that their interviewee will shout down the telephone, enquiring why they are asking such stupid questions and to stop wasting their time!

But, to get over those negative nerves, it's important to break the task down into much smaller, more manageable, chunks. Think of them as mini short-term goals. Using your list of tomorrow's work, create a *detailed* list of what you need to do. What I mean by this is, break the job down into much smaller steps so that completing them becomes easier. So don't write:

Telephone interviewee for quotes for article.

Instead, make an easy-to-achieve list like so:

- ☺ Create a list of ten open questions to ask interviewee (beginning *what, where, when, how, why, who*).
- ☺ Type them up to make them easy to read.
- ☺ Clear space on desk to make room so that I can take notes comfortably.
- ☺ Telephone 01632 960458 and ask questions!

Breaking the job down into much smaller, specific steps makes them more attainable and therefore increases the chances of you actually tackling them. You are less likely to procrastinate. Add as much detail to each step as you can. Listing the telephone number is a good example of this. If you'd plucked up the courage to make the phone call and then couldn't lay your hands on the telephone number, you would have the perfect excuse not to make the call, literally forcing you to put the job off until later!

So don't make it easy for procrastination to take over. A little thought beforehand can make all the difference. This is why my last job of the day is to jot down the list of things I need to do tomorrow. There are usually one or two easy things in the list that I can tackle when I first sit at my desk to get me started. But if there's one job there, which I know I don't like and will probably try to put off, I will spend the time now breaking it down into much smaller steps. That way, when I sit at my desk the next morning, I know that I will get that job done too. Procrastinators spend time thinking, but it's actions that get the job done. And writing is an action that we should all be aiming for!

Word count summaries

As writers, we are used to dealing with words, but we also have to deal with numbers. Word counts can be the bane of many a writer's life, particularly if your short story is 4,000 words long and the competition you are aiming it at only allows entries of up to 2,000 words! But as we've seen from the earlier sections about monitoring our short, medium and long-term goals; keeping a record of word counts helps us to measure whether we are achieving the goals that we set out to accomplish.

Since becoming a full-time writer, I've kept a daily record of the number of words that I've written. All that is required is a simple spreadsheet. This works for me because I enjoy tackling a variety of projects throughout my writing day. I update this spreadsheet every time I stop working on one project and before I move on to the next. This allows me to monitor the number of words I produce every day, week, month and year.

Date	Manuscript	Title	Word Count
18/01/XX	Workshop	Positively Productive 3747	
21/01/XX	Non Fiction Book	The Positively Productive Writer	1283
22/01/XX	Non Fiction Book	The Positively Productive Writer	1886
23/01/XX	Non Fiction Book	The Positively Productive Writer	717
25/01/XX	Article	Llanberis	830
25/01/XX	Non Fiction Book	The Positively Productive Writer	1248
28/01/XX	Blog Posting	Cut The C**p!	145
28/01/XX	Non Fiction Book	The Positively Productive Writer	442
28/01/XX	Article	Llanberis	137
29/01/XX	Article	Llanberis	1127

Above is a snapshot from my spreadsheet to give you an example. The first column records the date and you'll notice that the same date often appears more than once. This reflects the diversity of my workload throughout the day. The next column identifies the type of manuscript that I'm creating, such as a non-fiction book, an article, a short story, novel, letter, blog, whatever. The third column specifies the actual manuscript that I'm working on and demonstrates that I often spend several days working on the same project, but I don't always spend all day working on just one project.

The word count column follows next. This clearly declares how many words I've added to that particular project on each day and this helps me to monitor my own writing goals. A quick look at this shows that I too have my good days and my fan-blooming-tastic days! Look at 18th January! I really flew on that day didn't I? Yet on 28th January, I only managed 724 words, despite working across three different projects. What this spreadsheet doesn't record is the fact that I wasn't at my desk for most of the morning because I was out taking some pictures for an article. However, if you add the number of words produced across all seven days identified here, my total word count comes out at 12,562. That's the equivalent of 1,795 words every day. Looking at the bigger picture helps me to put the 28th January's relatively poor figures into perspective.

Although not on the example above, I have two more columns to the right of this table. The next keeps a track of the number of words written each month and the one after that keeps track of an annual figure.

If you're a bit of a whizz with spreadsheets then the simple table above will help you to extrapolate quite a bit of information. Adding some data sorting functions can allow you to ascertain how many words you've written in articles, short stories, non-fiction books etc., or how many words you've written in total for a particular project. Don't spend too much time establishing quirky facts and figures from your data. You'll merely be wasting valuable writing time! This simple list is enough to help me to monitor my own personal writing goals.

Quick Wins

The best way to remain positive as a writer is to be published from time to time. I know, I know, I know! If everyone had everything that they ever wrote published, then we'd all be permanently swanning around in a positive frame of mind! The point I want to make here is that ANY piece of published work will help you to keep your positive mental attitude, whilst you tackle the larger projects like novels, screenplays and other non-fiction books. I still get a kick from everything I have published and when I say everything, I mean EVERYTHING. That includes letters to a publication's letters page.

Readers' letters

As a writing tutor, one of the first ways of getting published that I demonstrate to my students is by writing a letter to a magazine's letters page. The reason for this is that many letters are relatively short, maybe 100 words, although some are fewer than 20 words. This means they're relatively quick to write. Many of the markets that ask for letters, like the daily newspapers and the weekly women's magazines, have a constant demand for such writing. Even better is that some of the paying markets pay extremely well. I once wrote a 105-word letter to the Sunday Express and it won me £300. How long did it take me to write? Well, if I allowed a total of half an hour to cover the editing process as well, that still equates to an hourly rate of £600. How positive is that?

In the UK, the most lucrative markets are the high circulation women's weekly magazines. The huge readership means that they can afford to pay better rates. Not all magazines pay the same rate, if anything at all. Some magazines don't make any payment for letters and many newspapers don't. Yet other magazines will only pay for the Star letter, while some will pay more for the Star letter and a little less for all other letters published.

Letters can be funny anecdotes, household tips, a disagreement with a writer of a letter in a previous issue, or to offer thanks for some advice given in a particular article. Editors love readers' letters because they give the publication a club-like feel and stimulate debate.

Here's a letter of mine that was published in the supermarket magazine *On the Road* for Tesco, which not only praised the company, but also provided a useful tip:

"It wasn't until a recent holiday trip from the Midlands to Scotland that I realised the full value of your website, www.tesco.com. Fed up with paying over-the-odds prices that the motorway service stations insist on charging for everything from petrol to a cup of tea, I decided to search your website for stores near the M6. It was brilliant. I paid a supermarket petrol price, had a break in the coffee shop and stocked up on provisions, all at Tesco's excellent prices."

For that I earned £25 in Tesco vouchers.

Editors will publish letters that criticise them, although take care here.

Critical letters that succeed in publication usually refer to a failure or a perceived failure by the magazine and offer the editor an opportunity to explain. Alternatively, critical letters give an editor an opportunity to express the other side of the argument, when there may not have been space for this in the original article. Below is an example of a critical letter I wrote, which was published in a photographic magazine:

"Dear Photoplus
It's great to see a magazine focussed on Canon camera users.
However, one thing I have noticed you have in common with the other photography magazines is a lack of explanation of certain

Photoshop [a computer software programme popular with photographers] *aspects. For example, in the Skills section you may tell us to set a brush tip to a radius of 15, or to sharpen at 85%. Yet we're never told why to use those particular numbers at that particular time. I appreciate that we can experiment ourselves, and even I can tell the difference between sharpening at 85% and 55%, but no one explains why to use 85% as opposed to 82%. Why use a brush radius of 15 and not 14? Enlighten us please. It will help to demystify Photoshop even further.*
Yours sincerely
Simon Whaley"

Whilst this may be seen as a critical letter, it does give the editor the opportunity to explain why they do what they do. And it still won me the Star Prize, a memory card for my camera worth over £50.

Editors won't publish letters by *disgusted of Doncaster, annoyed of Arizona, miffed of Mumbai,* or *sarcastic of Sydney* – you'll need to supply your full name and address, and sometimes they ask for a daytime contact telephone number.

As you can see, letters can become a nice little sideline. My letters have earned me money, gift vouchers and various prizes. I've won computer software worth £900, hiking shoes worth £100, bird boxes and books. And any prize that you don't like can be turned into cash by selling it on an online auction site. I know of one writer who uses all the money they earn just from writing letters to pay for their writing holiday every year. These quick wins can be financially rewarding and very beneficial.

When looking through a magazine or newspaper, instead of saying to yourself, *"Oh, that happened to me,"* or, *"That article has helped point me in the right direction,"* put your thoughts down on paper. Turn it into a letter.

Don't dash off your thoughts and click the Send button straight away – do some research.

☺ Look at the publication and examine how long the letters are. National newspapers will accept some long, well-argued comments of up to 400 words, whereas some magazines won't use anything longer than 150 words. If all the letters you read are shorter than 50 words, then your letter has to be that short too.

☺ Do the letters refer to articles in previous issues, or even previous letters?

☺ Are they light-hearted and chatty in style, or are they serious? How long are the sentences?

☺ Never send the same letter to several magazines. Editors don't like it – particularly if they are competing magazines with similar readerships. Readers don't like it either. It annoyed me when I came across it, so heavens knows what the editors thought. The same letter was published in two different writing magazines, in the same month. Now, as a subscriber to those magazines, I wasn't particularly happy about paying twice to read the same material!

Avoid sending letters to the letters page on headed notepaper if you are claiming to be a freelance writer. Editors want letters from their readers, not professional writers!

You can type your letter, but if it is short and your writing is clear to read, handwritten letters are acceptable. These days though, most publications accept reader's comments by email instead of by snail mail, and it's a much better (and cheaper) way of submission. If you're targeting a daily newspaper, then make sure you email your letter as early as you can, before lunchtime if possible. The earlier you send it in, the better chance it has of being used in the following day's issue.

Don't expect a rejection letter back. Some magazines will contact you (usually by email) but not all do. If you are using snail mail, only enclose a stamped addressed envelope if you are sending a photograph that you want returned. Pictures are often the clinching factor with publication. If you see pictures on the letters page, then try to include a picture with your letter. Sometimes, magazines pay more for the pictures.

Fillers

Fillers used to be small pieces employed to fill up a page in the days when printed material was produced using hot presses. These days, if an article isn't quite long enough, modern computer technology means that the text's font size can be increased, or pictures can be used to fill up more of the space. As a result, fillers are rarely used to fill up space.

What has happened is that magazines tend to have what I call *filler pages*. These are whole pages devoted to several shorter pieces. A fiction magazine may have a page of 60-word short stories, or a poetry page. A women's magazine may have page devoted to household tips, or stupid things that reader's husbands and partners do.

These sorts of pages are great to target because it's an excellent way of honing your writing skills. For a 60-word short story to work, you really have to make *every* word count! They may not pay much, but £10 here and £25 there becomes several hundred pounds during the course of a year. And that's on top of the kick you've had from being published.

Ideas for Letters/Fillers include:

☺ Things other people say to you.
☺ Things you overhear people saying – particularly children.
☺ Memories triggered by recent events.
☺ Your own strong views or opinions.

Personal opinion pieces

Whilst the vast majority of letters to a letters page are a personal opinion, often the restricted word limit means that a subject can't be tackled in detail. Step forward the personal opinion piece, which some magazines are now promoting, either as a Reader's Viewpoint or a Reader's Rant or an In My Opinion slot. The word length for these varies, but can extend from a couple of hundred words to nearer 800.

The joy with these pieces is that because they are based upon your own opinion, there's less research required. If there's one thing we're all good at, it's moaning, and many of these viewpoints are a perfect opportunity for a good moan! Instead of getting frustrated about something, get it off your chest and write it down! You'll feel better for it, particularly if it results in publication and a cheque. How's that for twisting a negative into a positive!

Reader experiences

Similar to the opinion pieces, the reader experience piece is becoming more widespread too. Just like the letter pages, these slots are intended for readers of the publications to submit material too. But writers are readers too, so why not get in on the act? It could lead to a quick publication, a quick win, a bit of money or a prize and that all-important positive publication boost.

I spotted in *The Observer* Sunday newspaper travel section a reader experience called My Crap Holiday. It was a short column of 400 words where readers were invited to submit a short anecdote about their worst holiday. So I did. It was easy enough to do, the full details and email address were at the bottom of the column. I wrote my first draft on the Sunday, put it aside until the following day, edited it and when I thought it was right, I emailed it across on Monday afternoon. The following Thursday I received an email saying that my piece would be used in the next issue of the paper. How quick was that? Publication within a week! I even won a small prize.

Such was the speed of this quick win (and the positive joy of being published in a national Sunday newspaper) I thought some of my writing students would be interested. I brought it to their attention and suggested that they had a go. And they did. In fact, over the following six-week period, my students managed to fill that slot in four of the weeks! It was great to receive the emails from them when they'd received their acceptance email. The positivity this gave them created a buzz between all of the students.

So, take a closer look at magazines and newspapers. Many of the weekend newspapers have similar reader experience slots. Some even offer payment instead of prizes. The great thing about these small pieces is that a first draft is achievable for many writers within a 30-minute writing slot. It's also a useful extra short-term goal to add to your goal list.

Networking

Staying positive as a writer can be achieved by networking with other writers. Writing is a solitary business and, because of that, there's no one to stop those niggling negative thoughts from becoming depressive left-brain analytical processes telling you to disconnect the keyboard immediately. DON'T! Instead, look for someone to talk to.

Networking is so important it is worth making it one of your writing goals. Not only can you use it to inspire you further, but you can also use it as a reward. Finished a piece early? Celebrate by telling someone! Go out and mingle with other writers. My career has certainly benefited from the contacts that I've made along the way.

Online

One of the easiest ways to do this is to join an online forum. Here you will be able to post questions asking for advice and support, as well as read about what other writers are experiencing. Realising that you are not alone helps to push back those negative feelings. Online forums can also be positively productive too. Writers Lorraine Mace and Maureen Vincent-Northam met on such a forum and ended up co-writing a book together. *The Writer's ABC Checklist* (Accent Press, ISBN: 978 1907016196) was written without the two of them meeting face to face until half an hour before they met the publisher!

A simple search on the Internet will reveal a plethora of such forums; some will provide feedback on the work you have produced. It's worth putting some effort into assessing these sites. Read other writers' work and consider its value. How impressed with it are you? If you're not impressed with the writing, the chances are you may not be impressed with the feedback. Remember, the whole point of this exercise is to remain positive!

Some useful networking sites and forums include:

- ☺ Writelink – www.writelink.co.uk
- ☺ My Writer's Circle – www.mywriterscircle.com
- ☺ Writing Magazine/Writers News Talkback – http://talkback .writers-online.co.uk/
- ☺ JournoBiz Forums - http://journobiz.com/forums/
- ☺ You Write On – www.youwriteon.com/
- ☺ Write Words – www.writewords.org.uk
- ☺ Writers Net – www.writers.net
- ☺ Writer's Digest Forums – www.writersdigest.com/ Community/
- ☺ Chillibreeze – The forum for Indian Writers – www.chilli- breeze.in/forums/

Writers' circles

"My name is Simon Whaley, and I am a writer." It's several years since I said those words, and sitting around in a circle with a group of other like-minded people was quite daunting. However, just like attendees at other self-help support groups, I was facing up to reality. The phrase meant two things. Firstly, I realised that I was respecting myself as a writer. If I didn't respect *myself* as a writer, how could I expect others to respect me in this way? Secondly, it meant that I respected the others as writers who could help me.

Now, I don't know what goes on inside anyone else's head (which is probably a good thing!), let alone that of another writer, but every day, I try to put down my own thoughts on paper. Sometimes it works. Sometimes it doesn't. It's those days when it doesn't that are the most isolating. That's when negativity creeps in and I need another writer to say, *"It's okay. It happens. Have you tried... ?"*

Within two minutes of sitting in that writers' circle, I was revealing some of my innermost thoughts. Thoughts I wouldn't have dreamt of revealing to close family or friends. Yet all around me were people who knew what I was going through. They understood those thoughts and, best of all, they'd had them too. Suddenly, I didn't feel isolated any more. The negativity fell away. It was so liberating!

I was lucky. Writers' groups are made up of individual writers. Therefore, each group is unique. You should appreciate that not *every* writers' group is right for *every* writer. You need to try before you buy. Go along to a few meetings to see if you like everyone. Do the meetings inspire you, or do they bore you? If they bore you, then get out of there quick and look for another group! A bored, uninspired writer is not a positively productive writer.

I also want to make another point clear. A writers' group is not a writer's panacea. They do not know the answer to everything, but often they can point you in the right direction. Occasionally, they may have a guest speaker, a writer who has succeeded and suddenly you have access to someone you wouldn't normally have come across whilst slogging away at your computer. And because you're amongst friends, you may even ask those questions that you wouldn't have the confidence to ask at a larger literary event, packed with hundreds of other non-writing people.

Alternatively, writers' groups can offer constructive criticism on your work. Writing in that isolated ivory tower means that you get too close to those precious words to realise what does and doesn't work. Sometimes other writers can remind you of that and suggest how to improve things. It's still your responsibility to decide which pieces of advice you're going to accept, but which is a better position to be in? One where you have no feedback, or one where you have several ways in which you can improve your work? If three or four people all say the same thing, then it would be foolish to dismiss them. It's often this criticism that can make such a difference. Friends and family don't think like writers, so they can't judge like a writer. As a result, they don't give feedback like a writer.

I still go to that same writers' group now and I also go to another one. I enjoy the regular fix with my fellow writing friends. They help me, just as much as I help them. We feed off each other. We pass on hints and tips and warn of scams or late payers. And if there's ever a problem in between meetings, I only have to pick up the phone or send an email. If I need a confidence boost, I know which of my circle friends to go to for support. That network helps me to keep things in perspective.

I mentioned at the beginning of this section that going to a writers' circle sends a strong psychological statement to your brain. It shows that you are beginning to respect yourself as a writer, because you're making the time and effort to go to a regular meeting. It means that YOU are taking YOUR writing SERIOUSLY. It also sends a clear signal to everyone else in the household. Those couple of hours on a Tuesday night or a Saturday morning are important to you. As a result, they will learn to respect that time as YOUR time. Going to a writers' circle will help your family and friends to respect you as a writer. That is another positive step.

A writers' group has given me confidence. I've shared my joys and my disappointments. When I share a disappointment, my despondency lessens. When I share a joy, it is always magnified. My name is Simon Whaley and I *am* a writer. However, I wouldn't have succeeded without the help and support from all of my friends in my writers' group. I would urge any writer to find one. It could be one of the most positive steps you ever take.

To find a group in your area, start by making enquiries at your local library, or your local evening class provider. Many groups start because creative writing courses at evening classes finish at the end of term and everyone wants to continue meeting. Some have forged friendships and have a better understanding of each other's writing style. If your local authority has an Arts Development Officer, they may be aware of groups in your area. Alternatively, search online:

UK Groups
☺ www.writers-circles.com/links.html
☺ www.nawg.co.uk.

USA Groups
It is best to search the Internet for groups in your local state.

Australian Based Groups
☺ www.sawc.org.au/groups/ (South Australian Writers Groups)
☺

http://www.actwriters.org.au/resources/writers_centres.sh tml (links to groups across Australia)

New Zealand Groups
☺ www.authors.org.nz/ (search for Writers' Groups under Writers Resources)

National Association of Writers' Groups
If there isn't a writers' circle or group in your area, you can still get some of that buzz and excitement by joining the National Association of Writers' Groups (NAWG). Individuals can join as Associate Members, wherever they are in the world. I'm an associate member and I bullied my writers' circle into joining too, which means that I'm a member twice! Membership entitles you to free entry to their annual set of competitions (and there's usually a wide range of categories ranging from poetry, non-fiction, short story, monologue, radio play, the list goes on), and a copy of their bi-monthly magazine *Link*, which has a great club-like feel to it.

If you're looking for a writers' circle, their website (www.nawg.co.uk) lists all of their group members, along with the relevant contact details. The website also lists details of a few international writers' groups who are members of NAWG.

Start your own

If you can't find a convenient group in your area, then why not start your own? You don't need a big room to start with. Many groups meet in a member's home, or in a quiet corner of the local bar.

The solitary nature of writing enables you to lose the perspective of a problem, much more easily. Within minutes, what is in reality a minor setback can swamp you with negativity and completely demoralise you. Don't let this happen. Build up a network of friends who can help you put things into perspective. They can help you retain your positivity.

Writing organisations

Being a member of a professional organisation not only gives you confidence, but it can be a great support system. It also shows third parties that you are professional in attitude. I am a member of the Society of Authors and the Outdoor Writers and Photographers Guild. I state this on my letterhead and my emails when approaching editors.

If you work in a large multinational company then you have a network of departments to call upon whenever you have a problem. If the computers go down, then you call IT. If you have a legal query, you can see someone in the legal department. If you have a problem with a customer who isn't paying up, then you go and speak to the credit control team in accounts. But, when you're sitting in your own writing space, on your own, and you encounter a problem, you suddenly feel immensely vulnerable. This vulnerability leads to insecurity and negativity. That's when you start withdrawing into yourself and stop taking any actions that you perceive may be risky, when in actual fact, they're not.

Being a member of a larger writing organisation can help you to overcome this insecurity and return you to a more confident, positive frame of mind. Whenever I've received a contract from a publisher, I've used the Society of Author's contract vetting service. It is free to members and has saved me many solicitor bills. When my first book, *100 Ways For A Dog To Train Its Human* was published, the contract seemed longer than the book! And the Society recommended that I asked for a few amendments to be made to the contract too. I remember being so nervous of doing this. It was my first book contract after all! I was glad that someone was prepared to give me a contract. The last thing I wanted to do was upset them by saying I didn't like the contract. But, these were my negative nerves kicking in. The Society explained to me that the changes I was asking for were quite minor in the grand scheme of things and the fact that I had consulted with the Society demonstrated that I was dealing with the contract in a professional manner. In the end, I had nothing to worry about.

I went back to the publisher, explained the queries that the Society had raised and they issued a revised contract. Contrary to what my imagination was conjuring up, nobody died, nobody pulled out of the contract and nobody rang me up to give me a mouthful of verbal abuse and ending with the words *"don't you realise that we're doing you a favour?"*

One of those queries did amend the financial side of the contract in my favour, once book sales reached a certain threshold. I don't think the publishers anticipated that the book would ever reach that threshold – I certainly didn't – but it did, which meant that listening to the Society's advice was the right thing to do financially too.

Such organisations will keep in touch with you through the various newsletters and magazines they produce, all containing useful, pertinent and important advice. They may even provide a mechanism for you to get more work. I've received commissions from editors who've found me through the Outdoor Writers and Photographers Guild website.

Consider joining any appropriate organisations that you can. Yes, they may be expensive, but give them a go. If, after a year's membership, you've felt that the organisation hasn't been beneficial, then resign, but try another one. One thing I've discovered is that most writers are willing to offer advice and support to any other writer if they can, particularly those who are members of the same group.

There are numerous market listings books aimed at writers, which identify all the various support groups that exist, including the Guild of Travel Writers, the Guild of Beer Writers, the Romantic Novelists Association, the Crime Writers Association, and so on, so it's not necessary for me to list them all here. There are several online databases (some require a subscription) that will also give you this information, including:

- ☺ Writers' & Artists' (UK) – www.writersandartists.co.uk
- ☺ Writer's Digest (USA) – www.writersdigest.com
- ☺ The Australian Writer's Marketplace – www.awmon line.com.au

Don't think you're not good enough to join these organisations! Guilds or groups may have some famous names as members, but that shouldn't put you off! Many groups offer associate or partial membership to new writers, or those who don't have a track record in their desired speciality. Often this means that the membership fee is lower too. This may mean that you don't have the right to vote at Annual General Meetings, but you'll still have access to most of the information and advice services, which is the real reason for joining. And some organisations, like the Society of Authors, run networking groups across the country, giving you access to real, live people at times too!

Writing may be a lonely occupation, but it is easy to feel part of a writing community.

Workshops / Seminars / Holidays

Here's an idea that is both a goal AND a reward. If you have never been to a writer's convention, holiday, course or seminar, then YOU ARE missing out. I GUARANTEE that you will return home from one of these events feeling immensely optimistic!

Set yourself the goal of attending at least one *every* year. More if you can afford it. Even better, set it as a goal, but use it as a reward for completing another big project if you can. Do your research though. There are a variety of courses, seminars and workshops across the country and they may not be right for you at every stage of your writing career.

If you are looking for a break surrounded by other writers (and I'm talking hundreds here), where you have an opportunity to go to a variety of workshops on different subjects, then investigate the follow:

UK Conferences/Holidays

☺ The Writers' Holiday at Caerleon, Wales (end of July) – www.writersholiday.net. Set on the University Campus at Caerleon, near Newport, Wales, this operates over five days, arriving on a Sunday afternoon and departing the following Friday lunchtime. During the mornings you can attend a series of workshops, from a wide choice. In some afternoons there are lectures and on one afternoon there's an opportunity to relax on a choice of three coach trips. Then there are a series of lectures in the evening. Lectures sounds grand, but in fact it feels more like a friend standing up and chatting with everyone. When I was invited to Caerleon to deliver an afternoon talk, I certainly felt as though I was talking to a group of friends. The last night of the holiday ends with a spectacular performance from a local Welsh Male Voice Choir. It's up to you which sessions, workshops, lectures or events you attend; you can pick and choose and make the most of what you want.

☺ The Writers' Summer School, Swanwick, Derbyshire (early August) – www.wss.org.uk/. Set at the Hayes Conference Centre over six days, there are selection of courses, workshops and talks taking place during the day, and then a selection of after-dinner talks in the evening. And if that doesn't tire you out perhaps the dancing, disco or bar will! Just like Caerleon, it's up to you to choose which events you go to, although the best piece of advice people gave me was don't try to go to everything. You can't. Make the most of what you can do.

☺ NAWG Open Festival of Writing – (location varies) – www.nawg.co.uk. A long weekend, but immensely productive! After arriving on Friday afternoon, it's an evening of getting to know everyone, followed by workshops on Saturday morning and afternoon, and opportunity for some one-to-one tutorials, ending with the gala dinner in the evening. It's here that the winners of the NAWG Writing Competitions are announced in a suitably Oscar/BAFTA ceremonial style! Sunday morning offers another workshop opportunity before making your way home after lunch.

☺ Winchester Writers' Conference, Winchester (end of June/Beginning of July) – www.writersconference.co.uk. A long weekend, which can be extended into a week of workshops. Stay for the weekend, the week, or just book for a workshop on one day.

☺ Festival of Writing, York (end of March) – www.festival-ofwriting.com. Another long weekend attended by agents, publishers, editors and published writers, offering workshops, seminars and even short one-to-one sessions with agents and book editors.

American Conferences/Holidays

- ☺ Southern Writers' Conference, three conferences held throughout the year in San Diego, Los Angeles and Palm Springs. For more information visit www.writersconference.com
- ☺ Central Ohio Fiction Writers Conference – a two-day event of lectures and workshops from writers, publishers, and agents. www.cofw.org/conference.html
- ☺ Bread Loaf Writers' Conference – four days of events and workshops in Middlebury, Vermont. http://www.middlebury.edu/blwc
- ☺ Sewanee Writers Conference – two weeks in Tennessee – visit www.sewaneewriters.org/

Australian & New Zealand Conferences/Holidays

- ☺ Australia Romance Writers Conference – a two-day event in August, which moves around the country each year. Visit http://romanceaustralia.com/conference.html for more information.
- ☺ New Zealand Foodwriters Conference – held in October each year and organised by the New Zealand Guild of Food Writers. www.foodwriters.org.nz/conference.htm
- ☺ Romance Writers of New Zealand Conference – held annually, every August. http://www.romancewriters.co.nz/conference/

Any of these breaks are excellent morale boosters. Take an empty address book with you to any of them and you'll return home with it full of new contacts – all friends. The company is excellent. Well it would be, because you're with like-minded people! If you're in full-time employment, treat these as a holiday where you'll actually get some writing done. If you are fortunate enough to be a full-time writer, then treat these breaks like work, but away from the office.

There are other holidays out there, targeting specific aspects of writing. One of the most well-known in the UK is the Arvon Foundation (www.arvonfoundation.org/) which has four venues dotted around the UK. Most courses run from Monday afternoon through to Saturday morning and numbers may be relatively small, fewer than 15. Two professional writers and a guest writer, who pops in during the week, lead the courses. The Arvon Foundation courses attract high calibre tutors, including writers such as Deborah Moggach, Lynne Truss, Maggie O'Farrell, Simon Brett and Willy Russell. They offer a brilliant opportunity to spend quality time with a well-known professional writer. Bursaries are available for those on low incomes, but treat it as a reward too. For example, if you want to write a novel then make one of their novel courses the reward for finishing the first draft of your tale. That way, not only will you get professional help on how to edit your novel, but the course will also give you a deadline for completing that first draft. Achieve that, and you've earned your right to be on that course, no matter what the cost!

Ty Newydd, once the home of the early 20th Century British Prime Minister, Lloyd George, is the National Writers' Centre for Wales (www.tynewydd.org/). It hosts a variety of courses, ranging from poetry to radio and children's writing to creative non-fiction at its 16th century property in Criccieth, Gwynedd.

In Australia, Varuna, the Writer's House is the country's only national writers' centre. More details can be found at www.varuna.com.au/ including details of the retreats and courses available.

A flick through any of the writing magazines (more on them later) will reveal a plethora of other breaks and courses. If you're interested in a particular genre, such as plotting the novel or writing short stories, your chances of finding a suitable course are high. And such holidays needn't be in your home country. Go abroad and immerse yourself in a completely different culture! It will heighten your senses and give you a more positive experience.

If you can't find the time for a week's break, look out for day workshops or seminars. These are often held as part of a literary festival and are an excellent way to boost your esteem. Remember, this is a learning experience, so consider it as training or personal development. If you're employed by a large company, you're probably used to sorting out a training plan for the year ahead enabling you to further develop your career. Simply think of these workshops and seminars as your training programme for your writing vocation.

Look out for courses and seminars advertised in the writing magazines, or search the Internet. Prices vary depending upon who the tutor is and whether lunch is included, but just like any of the other holidays and get-togethers, they are an excellent networking opportunity.

Do-it-yourself retreats

Both the Arvon Foundation and Ty Newydd offer retreat weeks. These are where there is no formal tutoring, but you can stay in the properties with other writers and work on your own project at your own pace. It's an opportunity to withdraw from the pressures of daily life and concentrate on your own writing in a suitable environment. However, if you're not ready for meeting other writers in this sort of setting, or don't have the time for a week's break, why not organise your own retreat, just for you?

A retreat is an opportunity to get away and immerse yourself in writing. It is NOT a holiday. A holiday is time to unwind, chill out, and relax. A writer's retreat is *your* opportunity to escape from day-to-day pressures and create some time for *you*. For YOU to WRITE.

Everybody's family situations are different, so a writer's retreat should be individual. You could leave the family on a Saturday morning and return on Sunday evening. It could be a longer weekend, or even a week if you have a really under-standing partner. The longer the period, the greater the opportunity is to be more productive. Whatever you can begin with, make sure you do it. When you've done it once, I guarantee it won't be the last time!

The best way to retreat is to book some self-catering holiday accommodation. Don't travel too far, you want to write, not travel. Self-catering accommodation can be very cheap outside the main holiday season. It is also perfect because you're the boss. YOU dictate what happens when. If you want to write from 2pm until 10pm you can. Being forced to adhere to a strict mealtime in a hotel or guesthouse can interrupt your flow adversely. So, if you want to pick at small amounts of food all day, you can. Or you may want to treat yourself by driving to the nearest fast food outlet and bringing back dinner in a bag. If you want to eat out at a bar with the locals, you can. Self-catering opens up the options for you. It's flexible.

There are various ways to find self-catering accommodation. If you are restricted to time and travel look in your local newspaper or regional magazine in the classified section. Don't forget your local Tourist Information Centre. If you want to travel further a field, search the self-catering accommodation agencies on the Internet. These include:

UK Agencies

- ☺ www.cottages4you.co.uk (National)
- ☺ www.helpfulholidays.com (Devon, Cornwall, Somerset & Dorset)
- ☺ www.wales-holidays.co.uk (Wales)
- ☺ www.heartofthelakes.co.uk (Lake District)
- ☺ www.northumberlandcottages.com (Northumbria)
- ☺ www.scothols.co.uk (Scotland)
- ☺ www.unique-cottages.co.uk (Scotland)
- ☺ www.dales-holiday-cottages.com (Yorkshire Dales & Moors, Cumbria, Northumberland, Peak District and Scotland)

☺ www.peakcottages.com (Peak District)

☺ www.norfolkcottages.co.uk (Norfolk and North Suffolk)

If you really want to push the boat out and treat yourself to an idyllic setting, then why not have a house with history? Perhaps the atmosphere will be even more creative?

☺ www.nationaltrustcottages.co.uk (National Trust – England Wales & Northern Ireland)

☺ www.ntsholidays.com/ – (National Trust for Scotland)

☺ www.landmarktrust.org.uk (Britain, Channel Islands, Lundy, Italy and the USA.)

USA Websites

☺ www.villarenters.com/ (Canada and the USA)

☺ http://sunvillasdirect.com/usa/ (Canada, USA and Mexico)

☺ www.landmarktrustusa.org/ (vacations in historic American properties)

Australian & New Zealand Websites

☺ www.holidayhouses.co.nz/ (New Zealand)

☺ www.schacc.com.au/ (Queensland)

☺ www.makemystay.com.au/ (Australia)

Ireland Websites

☺ www.selfcatering-ireland.com/

☺ www.homefromhome.ie/

☺ www.rentacottage.ie/

To maximise the benefit of your retreat, try to take everything you need for your writing with you. If that's just a pen and paper, fine, but if you prefer working directly on to computer, take a laptop. Don't forget your ideas book and any relevant reading or research material that you've already collated. If this retreat is just for you, then this may be your only opportunity to spread everything out on the floor knowing that the dog won't put messy footprints on it, nor will your mother-in-law tidy it all up. This is YOUR opportunity to live life as YOU have always dreamed life as a writer would be.

When you are on your retreat use the time wisely. Remember, it is not a holiday. You have told friends and relatives that you are going away to write, so you'd better take some written stuff back with you! However, don't feel compelled to pick up a pen as soon as you've unpacked. Give yourself a chance to relax and unwind into the right frame of mind. Take your favourite music with you. Practise any meditation techniques you've recently learnt, or follow in my footsteps and go for a walk. Remember too, a writer is also a reader. Use the time for market research, read other novelists if you're tackling a similar theme, but don't sit and watch telly! (The Landmark Trust properties in the UK are probably some of the best for writers – they have no televisions or telephones and, in many, mobile phone coverage isn't brilliant!) If you fail to do any writing, it is only yourself who you are failing.

A writer's retreat needn't be just for you. But it ought to be just for writers. If you belong to a writers' group, see if anyone else is interested in joining you. This develops the idea by living with people who understand how you feel and will leave you alone to write. But they are also there if you need guidance, constructive criticism or feedback on a piece. Your writer friends will understand when you wake up with a great idea for a short story and need to write it that morning. Could you do the same at home? Would your family understand? I have retreated several times, both on my own and with other writers. They are some of my most productive periods and they boost my enthusiasm for my return home.

A writer's retreat is a means to escape. It's a way of rewarding your dreams by providing that sought after time. Use it wisely.

Do some writing. Then when you return you may find that you've created that habit of writing at a regular time each day, something that hopefully you'll be able to continue at home. When you can read what you've produced, then you'll know that YOU ARE a writer.

Confidence

What does all this networking do? It gives you confidence. One year, Vivien Hampshire, a successful short story writer and poet, came to the Writers' Holiday at Caerleon in Wales. She elected to do two of the courses; one on motivation, led by Solange Hando, and the other on writing for magazines, led by myself. Here's what Vivien had to say about what that networking opportunity led to.

"Before Simon's article-writing workshop session at Caerleon, I was quite content to be a fairly successful short story writer and a dabbling poet. The thought of writing and selling non-fiction pieces had never really entered my head, I suppose because I mistakenly believed that to do it effectively it was necessary to be an established expert in some field or other, and I wasn't!

Simon's enthusiasm and the general air of fun and optimism in the room soon changed all that. As we chatted, played a few games, and looked through stacks of magazines of all shapes and sizes, many of which I had never encountered before, I soon started to realise what a huge market exists for well-written articles and features on an enormous range of very general and easy to research topics, and in all styles – from the highly informative to simple quizzes and 'top ten' lists. It was also clear that virtually every magazine I studied carried pages and pages of non-fiction as opposed to the one or two pages of fiction that sometimes, but not always, crept in. And all those magazines need regular articles to fill their pages. They needed writers, just like me!

Before the course I'd only ever had three non-fiction articles published, but when I got back home I found that new ideas kept popping into my head. My job, my hobbies, people I met, things I saw in the press all started to produce a frightening array of possibilities that I could pull into shape and write about! By amazing coincidence and good luck, it was then that Writers' Forum (www.writers-

forum.com), *under a new editor, advertised the fact that they were open to ideas from new writers. So I rather cheekily emailed to suggest, not just one article, but a monthly column which would follow the ups and downs of a very ordinary writer – me! – on her quest to get out there, get published and make some serious money.*

It took a bit of to-ing and fro-ing and a couple of attempts to get the tone just right, but pretty soon the editor said yes and my new column, 'Barbados or Bust', was born. I posed for a 'dreamy-eyed' photo, which would appear alongside a picture of a beautiful beach in the titles. I came down from the ceiling where I had been floating ever since I got the job, and started work! The aim was to make enough money in a year of writing anything and everything (and taking the readers along with me every step of the way) to take me on a holiday, and no one knew whether I would make it to a wet weekend in Blackpool or a fortnight sunning myself in Barbados. Believe me, there's nothing like the possibility of very public failure to spur a person on, and during that year I managed to research and follow up plenty of new leads, approach new markets, and sell all manner of articles and stories I never would have written before. The year ended, I did get to Barbados, but I couldn't stop! The bug had bitten, and there were still so many avenues to try and a seemingly inexhaustible supply of ideas buzzing around me everywhere I went.

I followed up the Barbados quest with a new regular column in Writers' Forum, this time helping readers with the process of writing and selling a novel, and I have another monthly column in a nursery publication looking at how we can choose and use picture books to help young children talk about their fears and cope with new situations.

Lots of doors have opened up for me over the last couple of years, but only because Simon's workshop showed me they were there, and I found the courage to try knocking on them!"

If Vivien hadn't come away on that writers' holiday, she may never have had the courage to approach the editor at Writers' Forum magazine to ask for the column. And a year later, when that column came to an end, she then had the courage to ask the editor for another one! As Vivien says, since then, her non-fiction output has exploded, and there's no doubt now that she's a positively productive writer!

Confidence is the major battle we have to overcome when we're sat at our desks on our own. Without it we have nothing to defend ourselves with from the attack of self-doubt. This is why online forums and writers' circles can be so beneficial. I've had emails from co-members of the writers' circle that I go to asking for advice and support and once I've given it, they're off. They just need that final piece of support that says, "*Yes, you're doing it right.*" Once they've had that, their confidence has returned. And funnily enough, the ideas that they've pitched to editors after getting that confidence boost have been accepted.

One of my students sent a panicked email to me along with her third assignment. She'd done as I'd suggested and sent off her article that she'd written for her second assignment. She'd also suggested a series of three or four other article ideas on a similar topic to the editor when she'd made her submission. Her email to me was full of panic because the editor had come back to her and asked if she'd consider joining the magazine as a freelance editor with that topic as her speciality! She didn't think she was capable, especially as she had only just started the course. But I told her that the editor's acceptance of her article and offer of the editorship was a clear sign that the editor had confidence in her!

Opportunities like this do not come along frequently, so I suggested that she should seriously think about it. Yes, it would be scary to start off with, but then isn't anything unknown to us in life a little bit frightening? My student agreed to think about it and then a week later she emailed to say that she had accepted the offer. She now supplies articles to the magazine on a regular basis.

Similarly, another one of my students had been living abroad and, in order to get some writing experience on the tiny island where she was based, had agreed to produce a newsletter for the local Chamber of Trade. When she returned to the UK, someone suggested that she should apply for the role of an editor of a magazine for a writing organisation. At first she was nervous and asked for my thoughts on the matter. I reminded her that when she'd produced the Chamber of Trade newsletter, she was, in effect, the editor of the publication. Therefore she had editorial experience. So she applied for the job. And she got it. So you see, positivity and confidence work closely together, hand in hand. Have one and you'll have the other.

Literary Festivals

Make it a goal to go to at least one literary festival every year. There are hundreds that take place throughout the year in practically every country around the world. It's an excellent opportunity to go and listen to other writers. Tickets are reasonably cheap, some events may even be free. Sometimes it's a great opportunity to go and pick up tips from a favourite author, at other times it could be the perfect opportunity to pick the brains of someone in the industry. I've attended literary festivals where I heard writers like Fay Weldon, Roy Hattersley and Andrew Motion speak and I've also been to festivals where I've had the opportunity to ask crime writer Colin Dexter for advice about novel writing. At one festival I even managed to speak to an editor of a major publishing house and asked her for advice about submitting work to a publisher. Opportunities like that don't arise like that very often, but it's at festivals when they can happen. Literary festivals are a great place to network.

Get yourself added to the mailing lists of as many festivals as you can, so that when programme details are available, you can start booking up. Tickets for popular speakers go quickly, so speed is of the essence. The larger literary festivals include:

UK Festivals include:

☺ The Hay Festival – www.hayfestival.com – at Hay on Wye on the English/Welsh borders, held at the end of May, beginning of June.

☺ The Cheltenham Literature Festival – http://www.cheltenhamfestivals.com/literature – held in October.

☺ The Edinburgh International Book Festival – www.edbookfest.co.uk – held in August.

☺ Harrogate Crime Writing Festival – www.harrogate-festival.org.uk/crime/ – held in July.

Another excellent group of festivals held throughout the UK are those run by Ways With Words (www.wayswithwords.co .uk). They operate the Dartington Literary Festival near Totnes in Devon in July, the Southwold Festival in Suffolk in November and the Words by the Water Literature Festival in Keswick, Cumbria in February.

For a comprehensive list of festivals throughout the UK visit the British Council's Literary Festival website at www.british-council.org/arts-literature-literary-festivals.htm for a month-by-month breakdown.

USA Festivals include:

- ☺ Tennessee Williams / New Orleans Literary Festival – www.tennesseewilliams.net/ – held in March.
- ☺ North Carolina Literary Festival – www.ncliteraryfestival.org/ – takes place in September.
- ☺ Newburyport Literary Festival – www.newburyportliteraryfestival.org/ – takes place in Newburyport, Massachusetts in April.
- ☺ Washington National Book Festival – www.loc.gov/bookfest/ – September
- ☺ Baltimore Book Festival – www.baltimorebookfestival.com/ – held in September.

Australian and New Zealand Festivals Include:

- ☺ A good site listing numerous festivals is www.literaryfestivals.com.au/
- ☺ Melbourne Writers Festival – www.mwf.com.au – August
- ☺ Emerging Writers Festival – www.emergingwritersfestival.org.au – held in Melbourne in May.
- ☺ Byron Bay Writers Festival – www.byronbaywritersfestival.com.au – August
- ☺ Wanganui Literary Festival – www.writersfest.co.nz/ – September

☺ The Press Christchurch Writers Festival – www.chchwritersfest.co.nz/ – September

☺ Perth International Arts Festival – www.perthfestival.com.au/ – February

Irish Literary Festivals include:

☺ Dublin Writers Festival – www.dublinwritersfestival.com/ – June

☺ Cork Spring Literary Festival – www.munsterlit.ie/Spring_Literary_Festival.html – February

☺ Listowel Writers' Week – www.writersweek.ie/ – May

☺ West Cork Literary Festival – www.westcorkliteraryfestival.ie/ – July

☺ The Flat Lake Literary and Arts Festival – www.theflatlakefestival.com/ – August in Clones, Co Monaghan

☺ Dublin Book Festival – www.dublinbookfestival.com/ – March

Writing Magazines

Right. These are NOT a luxury, but a NECESSITY! (No, I'm not being paid by the magazines for saying that!) They are the best way to keep abreast of the variety of holidays, seminars, workshops and literary festivals going on, up and down the country. They are also an excellent source of news and information about various writing competitions and they are packed with immensely useful advice.

In the same way that a writers' circle or group becomes a regular weekly, fortnightly or monthly fix, so too does the next issue of the writing magazines. Respecting yourself as a writer means acting professionally about it. Keeping up to date with events in the writing world is important and the magazines are an important tool. No matter what industry you work in for your day job, there'll be a key publication aimed at people like you. The writing magazines are exactly the same thing. GET THEM.

Treat them as a reward mechanism too. When you've achieved one of your short-term goals for the day, give yourself a ten-minute break to read an article or two in them. Enter the competitions, write to the letters pages and get involved with them. YOU WILL benefit from doing so and, as a result, your writing will benefit too.

Remember that many magazines will offer worldwide subscriptions, so it's possible to subscribe to foreign publications too. This is a particularly good idea if you want to write for foreign markets.

UK Writing magazines include:
  ☺ Writers News / Writing Magazine – https://www.writers-online.co.uk/ – available in large newsagents or by subscription, these two-magazines-in-one offer in-depth news and practical articles. Readers can take part in

regular poetry and short story competitions.

- ☺ The New Writer – www.thenewwriter.com – available quarterly by subscription. Aimed at all writers, novelists, non-fiction writers, poets and short story writers, it has a good club-like feel.
- ☺ Writers' Forum – www.writers-forum.com – available monthly on subscription or from larger newsagents.
- ☺ Mslexia – www.mslexia.co.uk – A quarterly magazine for women writers aimed at complete beginners as well as seasoned professionals.
- ☺ Link – www.nawg.co.uk – A Bi-monthly magazine sent free to associate members of the organisation. Writers' Groups that are members are sent 3 copies per group.
- ☺ Freelance Market News – www.freelancemarketnews.com/ – There are 11 issues a year, detailing markets for articles, short stories, letters and fillers, both in the UK and abroad.

USA Writing magazines include:

- ☺ Writers' Journal – www.writersjournal.com/ – a bimonthly publication aimed at all writers.
- ☺ Writer's Digest – www.writersdigest.com/Magazine/ – 8 issues a year, packed full of information, particularly around the business of writing, market hints and tips and useful writing resources.

Part IV

A Positive Writer's Year – Strategies to Succeed

A Positive Writer's Year

To be a productive writer throughout the year, you need to be positive all year long. Some writers find this more difficult during the long winter months; others find the long sunny days of summer provide a perfect excuse not to be at the writing desk at all! Here's a monthly guide to remaining positive throughout the year, using some of the techniques that we've looked at in this book.

January

Firstly, go back to the start of this book and re-read Part I. January is the start of a new year, so it is the perfect time to set yourself some new writing goals. However, you now understand the importance of making them S.M.A.R.T. and breaking them down into short, medium and long-term goals, so be practical. Sit down and think about what you want to have achieved by the end of the year and work backwards. Break those goals down into manageable chunks.

Don't ditch the New Year Resolutions completely. Instead, think how your life's other goals can help to influence your writing. For example, why not resolve to enrol on an evening class during the summer and autumn terms this year? Or make a promise to go on a new course every couple of months to broaden your horizons. Or vow to visit a new destination every few weeks. Can you bring these newly-found skills or knowledge into your writing? Having something new to write about can be inspiring as well as encouraging. If you specialise in an area of writing (crime short stories, photography articles, camping articles, poetry), why not explore a new genre or subject matter? Expand your specialities. Don't just write crime short stories; learn how to write true crime articles as well. Stretch yourself and stretch your writing opportunities. At this stage in my writing career, I would classify myself as a non-fiction writer, but I've been learning about short story writing, particularly for the women's magazine market, and I'm now beginning to see signs of success here. I've had stories published here in the UK, Ireland and in Australia. By stretching myself and learning about a new genre of writing, I've opened up new writing markets and new opportunities for publication.

Next, treat yourself. Buy yourself a new notebook. Start the New Year with a new, pristine notebook. Hopefully, you'll start several more throughout the rest of the year, but make a specific point of starting a new one on 1st January.

Finally, have a clear out. Go through your desk, or writing area, and literally look at every piece of paper. Throw away what you don't need and put to one side everything that may be useful. You may be surprised at what you find. I've come across work that I started months ago and had completely forgotten about. The new start to the New Year gives me the impetus to finish it off.

January is the month of new starts. Make sure that you make plenty of them.

February

Roses are red,
Violets are blue
February's romantic
So why not fall in love with being a writer too?

If Valentine's Day makes February the month of love then why not take some time out and relight that burning desire you had in January for being a writer? This is the time of year when those big non-writing New Year Resolutions may have been broken; although hopefully, your short and medium-term goals are helping you to achieve your writing dreams! But it can still be too easy at this stage of the year to begin feeling a little despondent. Does that notebook on your desk, or the file saved in My Documents, feel a little unloved now? Was it the centre of your attention during those first few days of infatuation in January when the dream of being a writer kept your fingers lovingly caressing the keyboard? And then, did you wane as the month progressed and the procrastinating diversions of life's other love affairs begin to tempt you? The solution is to learn to fall in love again with your writing and enjoy a longer lasting relationship.

Start flirting again! It's those snatches of conversation, the double entendre, the discreet widening of eyes to the one that you fancy, which conveys so much information in that brief moment of teasing new love. Flirt with your notebook again. Write down the first half of an opening sentence, or the title of a short story, but be brief. Don't finish the sentence. Don't write the short story. Just write enough to show that you fancy the idea and will come back for more! Tease your notebook, but use it to tempt you to return for another sneaky peak liaison soon!

Enjoy the danger! Add a dash of extra excitement into your new relationship by keeping it concealed from others. No one must know! Treat your writing like an affair. Don't let anyone catch you and your notebook embracing a new idea. Hide in cupboards (stationary cupboards at work are perfect for this – all the right equipment is there!), take yourself off to beauty spots in isolated rural areas on cold, wet Wednesday mornings and let your car windows steam up. Or tell the family that you have a work conference out west but book a hotel by the sea instead. Be creative and think up excuses!

Get to know each other... intimately! Let your fingers gently stroke the spine of your notebook. Trace it from the top, tickle it gently, until you reach the bottom. Caress those rounded curves of the corners, gently tug at the outer sleeve and pull it back to reveal a pure, virginal, unblemished page. Now's your opportunity to have your wicked way with it! Scribble down your thoughts. Be honest. Don't hold back. Say what you mean. This is something between you and your notebook; no one else will know what you're writing about for the time being. Be free. Confide in each other. Share your secrets, but keep each other close to your heart.

Find excuses to be with each other for longer! Absence may make the heart grow fonder, but in our case, it encourages the brain to think that writer's block can drive a wedge between young love. The essence to keeping this relationship going is regular time together. And when you begin to find that your snatched moments are insufficient to quell your burning desires, then that's the time to start being creative again. Come up with ways to stay together for longer. Cut out that penultimate pint down the pub. Skip a couple of episodes of your favourite soap each week. Get the other half to wash and dry up. Bribe the kids into making their own packed lunches.

Declare your love to the world! There will come a point when you can't keep it a secret any longer. People will be whispering behind your back (but as an observant writer you will have already spotted this). Perhaps you have let something slip in an unguarded moment. Have you been spotted in an uncompromising position? Perhaps you have been discovered writing a short story when everyone else thought you were compiling a shopping list. When this point arrives, the golden rule is, never lie. Don't try to conceal the fact that you are a writer. Tell the whole world. Let them know. Shout your love from the rooftops!

As soon as you've done this, the world will begin to accept you as a couple. If you are invited to go somewhere, friends will understand that your notebook will want to come too. Good friends always experience a warm feeling in their heart when they see two people comfortable with themselves in front of everyone else. If an idea or thought strikes whilst you're out and about with friends, be brave. Get out your notebook and write it down. They won't mind. They will now appreciate that this is who you are. If an opportunity arises for you to go away on a writing course, your family will understand.

Learn to spice up your love life! Once you've rekindled your love of writing, don't let it fall into a relationship of habit. Inject some spontaneity! Go to a workshop on haikus if you're not a poet, try writing a short story if you're an article writer, or have a go at writing in dialogue if you like writing prose. The joy of writing is that with so many different genres and styles, there are just as many writing exercises as there are karma sutra positions! Go on, give it a go! You'll never know you're any good at erotic writing unless you try!

So, February is the month for finding some time for your other love – writing. Love your writing, and it will love you back.

March

March is the month for madness! Be spontaneous. The seasons are changing so change your routine. If you've created a series of daily walks, change them. Devise some new routes that you can stretch your legs as you walk along them. Look for new views that may inspire you. Absorb the impact of the changing scenery on your new routes.

Doing something completely different can also give you a huge psychological boost. Make sure that it is something completely unconnected with your writing, and book yourself on to a course. It needn't be evening classes at your local education centre; a one-day course can be just as beneficial. I booked myself on a bread-making course, which took place in an old watermill. Not only were we given a guided tour of the watermill and shown how the grain was ground down into flour, but we also had a go at making a variety of different breads. Lunch may have been a simple vegetable soup with a hunk of bread, but it was absolutely fantastic. Not only did I learn a new skill, but the experience may prove useful in my writing one day, whether it's for an article about such courses, or a character who bakes bread in a short story.

At this stage, don't look for what you can get out of the course for your writing, just look at it as a complete break. Give your brain a rest. I mentioned earlier how the brain is a muscle that can be trained to start writing at a set time each day with practise, but every muscle needs time for recovery, even if it is just for a few hours. Doing something completely different like this is a great way to rest and revitalise it.

April

Now that you're four months into the New Year, it's a good time to use the Doing a Fagin technique and keep a diary. Write down everything that you do for about two weeks and then analyse it to see what is working for you. What are you doing that produces good writing days? What affects you adversely? If you can, be spontaneous again, like you were in March, but do it in that two-week period to see what sort of effect this has on your writing. You may find it useful being spontaneous more frequently. (I won't say regularly because that takes away the spontaneity!)

Take a look at your word count summaries. Make sure that you're keeping count of every word that you write, whether it counts towards your novel, a short story, article, poem, or even a letter to the letters page of a magazine. A 20-word letter is still 20 words of writing! Total up your word counts for January, February and March. How does it look? Is it more or less than you imagined? Often it turns out to be far more because a negative mind tends to underestimate. I remember one month when all I could think about were the interruptions I had been subjected to day in, day out, and I was convinced that I'd achieved naff all! Yet when I totalled up all the words I'd written during that period I was surprised to find that I had actually produced in excess of 18,000 words! I've had much better months, but there it was in black and white, evidence that the month had not been completely wasted. That figure completely changed my perspective of the month.

May

If you haven't been to one already, track down a literary festival where you can get a literary fix. It doesn't have to be taking place this month, but search for any festivals near you and sign up online to the festival newsletter. That way, when the programme of speakers is finalised, you'll be one of the first to hear about it. When you see something you like, book a ticket. Treat yourself. Make it a reward for what you have achieved so far this year. Go and listen to a writer whom you find inspiring. Who would you like to emulate?

Attending an event like this and immersing yourself in a literary atmosphere can be hugely rewarding and you never know what might happen, or where it may lead. I attended a fascinating talk given by an editor from a major publishing house, which I found really useful and inspiring. Then, half an hour after it had finished, I found myself in the queue behind her at the refreshment tent. She kindly answered a couple of questions I had about the publishing industry and gave me some advice on a project I was working on, whilst we waited to be served. Now, that was positive!

Milling around at a literary festival allows you to absorb the atmosphere. You're with like-minded people. After the event, go and queue up for a drink and a bite to eat in the refreshment tent – you never know whom you might bump into! But take your time and do the writer-ly thing of sitting in a quiet corner somewhere, people watching. Eavesdrop on the conversations. Remember, for writers this isn't being rude – this is research!

It goes without saying now (it blooming well should do by this stage of the book) that you'll have your notebook with you. Not only should you be taking notes during the literary event that you've come to see, but jot down your thoughts and ideas as you sit here in quiet contemplative thought. Browse the bookshop, (there's always a bookshop at these events, even if it's just a table under an awning) and treat yourself to a book. Imagine yourself as a writer who's been invited to talk at a festival. How would you feel if you saw your books on the bookstall?

I was at a literary festival at Keswick, in the Lake District, one year and I'd been to a talk in the morning, but had a couple of free hours before going to another talk later in the day. The Keswick literary festival (Words by the Water) takes place in the Theatre by the Lake, and I sat in one of their café areas with my notebook. In the time between those talks, I drafted an article about the festival, which I later sold to The Lady magazine. Remember, you don't necessarily have to be in your dedicated writing space in order to write. If a literary atmosphere helps you to produce work, then shouldn't you be seeking more literary atmospheric moments?

June

Take a look at your S.M.A.R.T. goals and see how you're doing. You're nearly halfway through the year now, so hopefully you should be achieving some of your medium-term goals. It's important to review your progress to date and an ideal opportunity to remind yourself of what you have already achieved, whilst also allowing you to focus on what you still need to attain. By this stage of the year, you'll have forgotten what you achieved back in the first few months of the year. Perhaps you set yourself a target to write two short stories a month. Well, by the beginning of June you should have completed 10 so far.

However, our minds tend to focus on the negative aspects of life, so at the beginning of June all you may remember is the disastrous May you had when you didn't manage to write one short story. But if you stop now and take a wider perspective to look back over the rest of the year, you may remember that you managed to produce three short stories back in February and three in April in addition to your on-target months in January and March. This means that, despite the disastrous May (in your mind's opinion), you are actually still on target.

And if you're not on target, it isn't the end of the world. There's still time to turn things around and achieve that original goal by the end of the year. Take time out to think. Get your writing diary and make an appointment with yourself. Block out a morning or an afternoon, but don't have the meeting with yourself at your desk – take yourself off to some neutral territory. Go somewhere quiet where you won't be bombarded by emails or family members disturbing you. Time spent planning is never time wasted. If you can, take your writing diary with you and analyse the periods when you did achieve your goal of writing two short stories per month. What were the circumstances that allowed you to meet this goal? What's changed? What happened in those months when you managed to produce three? If family commitments mean that you can no longer devote as much time to writing, then is it any wonder that you're finding it difficult to meet this goal? Do you need to reassess it? Remember, a S.M.A.R.T. goal is one that is achievable. Slogging yourself out to achieve the unachievable is not the best way to remain positive and motivated! If your circumstances have changed since you originally set that goal then the chances are it is no longer achievable. Alternatively, is there anything you can do to reinstate those circumstances that enabled you to achieve the goal?

So, review all of your targets and adjust them accordingly, but be honest with yourself. Remember, goals need to be achievable but they should also stretch you. Reviewing your goals in this way means that hopefully, once you've carried out this exercise and re-adjusted them if necessary, you should be more positive looking ahead to the final six months of the year.

And don't forget your rewards! Have you claimed everything that you're entitled to? Even if you're in the middle of re-adjusting your goals, make sure you have enjoyed the rewards for ALL of those goals that you HAVE achieved. That will put you in better frame of mind!

July

Go away or make arrangements for a break in the near future. Make it *writing related* if you can, no matter how tenuous the writing link is. I've already provided details of some of the writers' conferences and events that take place. Alternatively, why not link a holiday with a literature festival? Travelling to a new part of the country not only adds interest (thus giving you ideas for travel articles or settings for more short stories) but the literary festival will give you your writing fix too. I remember going to the Ways With Words Literary Festival one year at Dartington in Devon. The weather was absolutely glorious, probably a little too warm if the truth be told, and as I wandered around the tranquil and beautifully-landscaped gardens of Dartington Hall, the atmosphere was wonderfully comfortable. There were people sunbathing on the manicured lawns, reading books they'd just bought from the book marquee. There were small groups of people huddled under shady tree boughs continuing the discussions they'd recently listened to in one of the author events. Wandering around, it was difficult not to feel literary. I found myself a shaded seat, sat down and scribbled thoughts and ideas in my notebook. And just as the weather made it uncomfortably warm, it would be time to escape into the refreshing Great Hall at the 14th Century building and sit in the cool alcoves of the large windows whilst listening to exciting writers like Fay Weldon.

If you're holidaying with family, a literary festival may not be practical, so go somewhere that will be of interest to all the family. Why not create your own literary trail? Visit the places that your favourite writers frequented or made famous, like James Herriot's Yorkshire, Ian Rankin's Edinburgh, James Joyce's Dublin, or Dan Brown's Washington. Absorb the surroundings, imagine how the writer has used the landscape to influence their consciousness and discover how the scenery may have inspired a plot line or story. And don't let bad weather put you off. What's more inspirational than witnessing a coastal storm with its dramatic thunder and haunting lightening?

Remember, writing isn't just about slaving away at your desk; it also involves getting out and about and experiencing life. Use your writing diary to analyse how well you are working too. The seasons have changed again, so has your writing pattern changed? If you're experiencing a good summer, perhaps it's too hot to work during the middle of the day. Working in the early hours of the morning or the later hours of the evening when it's cooler can be much more productive. Be as flexible as you can in this weather. You are more likely to meet your daily word count if you've written in the morning and late evening, than if you struggle to write during the midday heat.

And if July is your winter, are you making the most of the long, dark evenings? Consider getting out during the day and making the most of daylight hours (such as doing your daily walk), then write into the evening. Make your environment cosy, draw the curtains, put another log on the fire, turn down the main lights and switch on table lamps to cast a warm glow. Get yourself a drink, perhaps some nibbles, and sit down in front of your computer. Now you're set for a productive evening!

August

Find some new ideas. Ideas are the lifeblood of writers and so a writer without any ideas is not a positively productive one! Anniversaries can provide great ideas not only for articles, but also for short stories, poetry, novels and even letters. So, take a clean sheet of paper, write down the numbers 1 to 31 and look for an interesting anniversary event for each day of the month that may inspire you. For example, did you know that:

On 1st August 1971, during the second day of the Apollo 15 mission, astronauts discovered a rock that was thought to date back to the origins of the moon! Just imagine what it must have been like for the astronauts walking on the moon. How eerie did it feel being the only life-form on the planet? Or were they? What if you wrote a short story about aliens watching the astronauts?

On 2nd August 1984, the European Court ruled that a Surrey businessman had had his Human Rights breached when police illegally tapped his phone without his knowledge. So, what would you say to friends and relatives who rang you up, if you knew that your phone was tapped? Would it affect what you said? Taking the idea one step further, what if a character in a short story was struck by lightening one day, which meant that she could only answer questions truthfully? We may think that we're all truthful, but it's so easy to tell a little white lie in order to make life easy, isn't it? *"Does my bum look big in this?"* Hmmmm.

On 3rd August 1990, the temperature in Nailstone, Leicestershire, was recorded as 37.1C or 99F, breaking Britain's previous record hottest day, last seen in 1911. An article of weather related startling facts could easily result from this, whilst it might make the ideal setting for a short story about an ice-cream seller who ran out of ice cream!

The 4th August 2000 was the Queen Mother's 100th birthday. Did the Queen send her mum one of those cards that she sends to everyone who reaches their 100th birthday, I wonder. What can you create under the theme of celebration?

For many, August 5th 1962 will be remembered as the day that film star Marilyn Munroe was found dead. Death of a different kind happened on 6th August 1945 when an atomic bomb was dropped on Hiroshima, Japan. And on 7th August 1987, Lynne Cox, a 30-year old American woman, became the first person to swim across the Bering Straits that separate the USA from Russia. What would you do if you could choose to do something that nobody else had done before? What character traits do people like Lynne Cox have? How many novels can you think of that are based around a character who is driven to achieve what many see as unachievable?

So there we have a week's worth of anniversary facts, but look at the ideas it can generate. In fact, the idea of writing about startling facts that have happened during a particular month have proved useful to many article writers. I've read articles by writers who've told readers what else has happened on 25th December. Many people think that because it's Christmas Day everyone is at home with friends and family, but of course, the whole world doesn't celebrate Christmas and in some countries it is just an ordinary day.

This idea generation technique works at any time of year and there are several websites that will produce this information, although one of the best is the BBC's 'On This Day' site (http://news.bbc.co.uk/onthisday/). Inspiration may only be a date-related fact away.

September

September is the month when the world seems to go back to school, so why don't you? Instead of signing up to an evening class on a non-writing related topic, as I suggested earlier in the year, this time consider courses that will help you with your writing. Writing is a continuous learning process and the more you understand about what works and what doesn't, the more confidence you will have in your own writing.

Take this learning seriously. Sign up to a correspondence course. As someone who tutors students on a correspondence course I know from the comments that my students make that they like having the constructive feedback on their assignments. It's more practical than learning a writing skill from reading a book. If they have an idea for an article, they'll tackle it for their assignment, I'll mark it and point out what works and what needs improving, and this then gives them the confidence to send their work out into the big wide world.

A correspondence course isn't for everybody, although I believe that they are ideal for writers. In order to be a writer, you need to be a self-starter, someone who doesn't need to be constantly nagged in order to do something. Writers don't get published because they have an editor ringing them up everyday, asking where their text is. Writers get published because they sit down and write the words and then send them off, without being told to. And it's the same with a correspondence course. You tutor won't ring you up asking where your next assignment is. You need to be focussed and self-disciplined enough to sit down and tackle the assignment in the first place.

Writing correspondence courses are provided by a range of companies including:

- ☺ The Writers Bureau, Sevendale House, 7 Dale Street, Manchester, M1 1JB. www.writersbureau.com.
- ☺ The London School of Journalism, 126 Shirland Road, Maida Vale, London, W9 2BT. www.lsj.org/
- ☺ Writers News Home Study Courses, Fifth Floor, 31-32 Park Row, Leeds, LS1 5JD. www.writers-online.co.uk/Home-Study/
- ☺ Australian College of Journalism, Level One, 1 Waltham Street, Artarmon NSW 2064, www.acj.edu.au/
- ☺ The New Zealand Institute of Business Studies, PO Box 51811, Auckland 2140. http://nzibs.co.nz/

Another reason why some students like a correspondence course is because they don't meet their tutor! You are less likely to take long-term offence from written criticism, than you are if it is face to face. That's why some people don't like reading their work out at a writers' group or in an evening class. A negative, insecure writer may feel that the advice being given face to face is personal criticism, rather than constructive criticism. I'm not saying that written criticism won't make you cross; but because there is nobody else in the room, you are more likely to learn from it, when you've calmed down! And if criticism is easier to accept, then you're more likely to consider the feedback that you're being given and act upon it.

Of course, you can always use this as the start of a much bigger learning curve. The Open University runs creative writing courses, many of which begin in September. Study takes place using course materials, as well as through online tutor-group conferences. You may also be given the opportunity of corresponding online with other students on the course, or possibly even meeting up at one of the OU's 13 local centres dotted around the UK. Tackling each course can offer you points or credits, which you can then put towards studying a degree in a particular aspect of writing or any other subject.

The Open University can be contacted at PO Box 197, Milton Keynes, MK7 6BJ, or online at www.open.ac.uk.

Alternatively, why not contact your local university or further education establishment to see what courses they offer?

When September approaches, consider what you might learn, from going back to school. (And enjoy going to the stationers beforehand and buying all the important Back to School stationery that you'll need!)

October

If you haven't done so within the last two months, this is an ideal time to undertake another diary exercise. Analyse your writing days to assess what is and isn't working now, particularly as the day lengths are changing once again. Think back to the television experiment Julie undertook. Instead of slipping in front of the television as soon as you draw the curtains, could you slip in front of laptop instead? If our habits change at this time of year, try to encourage the change to be a positive one!

As well as looking back with the diary, October can be a great time to look forward too. A new year is just around the corner, so start thinking about which projects you might want to develop. Don't worry too much about specific goal setting – that's the job for next January. But allow yourself the time to dream. If you've been setting goals and rewarding yourself for what you have achieved over the past few months, you will by now know what you are capable of producing as a writer. What might have been seen as completely impossible in the past may now look possible. So, will next year see the start of that novel you've promised yourself, or that non-fiction book? What about a regular column in a local magazine, newspaper or parish newsletter?

What about foreign markets? Have you sold a short story and realised that it could be reworked for another magazine in a completely different country? Is it possible to sell different rights in the travel article of yours that was published earlier in the year? How else can you build upon this year's successes? Has that competition win inspired you to enter more competitions next year? Why not increase your target?

It doesn't matter what your writing dreams may be, write them down somewhere safe for next year. Put them in your notebook!

November

The best deadline is one set by someone else. Having created your own short, medium and long-term goals, it can be tempting to think that if you don't meet them, it is not the end of the world. After all, nobody dies. True. The only person it affects is you. And whilst you may think that nobody dies, there is *something* that dies... YOUR dream. If you're the type of person who finds it difficult to meet their own deadlines, why not have a go at meeting someone else's? November is the perfect opportunity because it is NaNoWriMo, or National Novel Writing Month. The challenge is to write 50,000 words of a novel in a month. Starting at one minute past midnight on 1st November, you have up until midnight on 30th November to complete 50,000 words. There are several reasons why this project may work for you.

- This isn't your deadline, it's the NaNoWriMo deadline. All around the world there are over one hundred thousand writers attempting to meet this goal. Not only are you in competition with yourself, but with other writers too. This camaraderie can give you the incentive to continue through to the end of the month. It's a race and if you cross the finishing line, your name will appear on that list of achievers. Online forums give you access to other writers' problems and thoughts during the event, so there's not the usual feeling of isolation that many writers face.
- Perfection goes out of the window. With such a tight deadline, there isn't time to produce perfect prose. This isn't the point of the exercise. The whole aim is to get the bulk of a first draft of a novel written. A lot of it will be rubbish, but as we've already seen, rubbish can be edited, honed and improved. The tight deadline effectively gives you the permission you need, to write rubbish.
- NaNoWriMo allows you to use the goal setting techniques in this book in several ways. You can use it, for example, to reach the 50,000-word target in 30 days. The long-term target is to write 50,000 words in a month. This produces a medium-term weekly target figure of 11,667 words, and a short-term daily target of 1,667 words. However, you could also use NaNoWriMo as a medium-term target in itself. If your goal is to write an 80,000-word novel, you could set yourself the long-term goal of having a novel written by the end of March. Medium-term goals may include spending March editing the second draft, using January

and February to edit the first draft, and having the first draft finished by the end of December. The end of NaNoWriMo on 30th November is, therefore, just one of many medium-term targets, with 50,000 words produced, leaving you with 30,000 words to produce in December. (You can relax a little in December, but not a lot!) Your short-term goals remain as your daily word counts. This way, you are using NaNoWriMo as a means of getting your project completed, rather than making NaNoWriMo the project itself.

- NaNoWriMo is a concept that non-writers understand; therefore, you are more likely to be taken seriously. If you tell family and friends that there is a competition taking place throughout November to see how many writers can produce 50,000 words within the month and you're going to have a go, they are more likely to accept your project. In fact, they may even encourage you, as they ask about your progress. Family and friends find it easier to accept that you may not be around much during November. For them, November is just a month, a little over four weeks. It's hardly any time at all. And whereas before, when you disappeared into a quiet room in the house for a couple of hours each night and no one really knew what you were doing (because you never showed your work to any of them), with NaNoWriMo, they can visit the official website (www.nanowrimo.org) and find out more about the event for themselves.

- NaNoWriMo has few rules. To take part, you should go to the website, www.nanowrimo.org and register. You'll then be sent details of how to record your daily word count figures. You can use your usual word processor programme on your own computer to take part. On 30th November, you have to copy and paste your text into the NaNoWriMo counting robot, which verifies the word count. Obviously, repeating the same word 50,000 times is not allowed. That would be cheating in all senses of the meaning! The only other main rule is that the 50,000 words must be new words. You can't use the 25,000 words you've already produced for your novel. November is about brand new words only!

You may find that NaNoWriMo helps to kick-start your regular writing habit. By the end of November, you and your family and friends will be used to you going off and doing some writing. Whilst you may not be able to continue on a daily basis writing for as long as you did during November, family and friends may accept you more as a writer now, particularly if you achieved the 50,000-word target.

This exercise also demonstrates that when you allow yourself to write imperfect prose, it is surprising what can be achieved. And if you can do it in November, then there's no reason not do it for the other 11 months of the year, is there?

December

And so we come to the final month. You are only a matter of days away from achieving your annual goals, if you haven't already. Yes, that's right, you may already have achieved many of your goals. Concentrate on the ones that you haven't achieved to date, for one big final push.

And in those final few days of the year, stop and look back at what you have achieved. Don't watch those end-of-the-year television review shows that are always on now, do your own review. Look at what *you* have achieved over the past few months. How many of *your* goals did you meet? How many did you exceed? Were there any that you failed to meet? Don't worry if you failed a couple. I look at that as confirmation that you set yourself enough goals to stretch and challenge yourself. If you met every goal that you set yourself last January, perhaps you should be asking whether you pushed yourself hard enough? Could you achieve more next year?

Be proud of what you HAVE achieved in the last 12 months though. Because if you hadn't set yourself those initial goals way back in January, you may not have achieved half of what you *actually* managed this year. This is when I look back at my word counts. I tot up the total number of words written each month, and then I add up the twelve monthly totals. The size of the number may surprise you. This is when the power of recording even the smallest number of words written during a writing session really shows its strength. Those little footsteps of 20 words here, 48 words there, and another 17 words in that five minute period between getting back from doing the shopping and leaving to pick the kids up from school really do add up into a journey of a thousand miles.

Take time to flick through your notebooks. (Note the plural!) Hopefully, as the year has progressed, you'll have filled a couple. Stop now and just turn a few pages, stop and read what you've written. Be proud of yourself. *You* wrote that. *You* filled all of those pages. Last January, those bits of paper in those notebooks were blank. They had not been filled with any of your thoughts, ideas and inspirations. Heck, they may not even have been purchased back then! Now they are a testament of your writing year.

Check that you've claimed all of your rewards. As the month draws to a close you should be achieving many of your bigger, longer-term goals, so wallow in the pleasure of rewarding yourself with those bigger, long-term rewards that you promised yourself.

Did you have any publishing success? If so, add it to your portfolio folder. Keep cuttings of published articles, short stories and poems. Now stop and look through it. YOU did that. This time last year, you hadn't.

Review your booster card. What else can you add to it now?

Are there any more writing successes that should included? You must add them. It's *this* year's achievements that will help you through next year's low points. Write them on your booster card to remind you of what you achieved this year and reinforce the message that YOU CAN do it, because YOU HAVE done it before. If YOU HAVE done it once, YOU CAN do it again.

Congratulations. You have now achieved a full year of writing and have a whole new year of new writing to look forward to. I wonder where it will take you? There's only one way to find out! Enjoy.

A Positive Farewell

Every writer's journey of a thousand miles is different. We all have our own individual destinations that we're aiming for in life. It may be a short story, an article, a novel or a poem. Yet, just like any other journey, there will be times when we are all travelling along the same section of motorway. It may be the same road, but we'll be turning off it at different points and continuing towards our own personal goals.

I hope this book has helped you along that motorway section. We all face jams and trouble spots in our writing journeys, sometimes we even get caught up in the same piece of congestion. But instead of shaking your fist angrily at the car in front, honking your horn, or getting out and pacing up and down the road whilst everything is at a standstill, I'm confident I have shown you that, with a small diversion, we can soon be on our way again. The shorter the hold-up the better, because it's imperative we get going on our journey as soon as possible. That way, we'll remain positive.

So share your success. Tell everyone! TELL ME! Drop me an email at contact@simonwhaley.co.uk or tweet me on Twitter at @simonwhaley. I'd love to hear which sections of this book have inspired you the most and what you have achieved.

Let me leave you with one final thought. Remember what I said about our creative right-brain and our logical left-brain? Studies suggest that it is our *creative right-brain* that deals with *negative emotions* and our *logical left-brain* that processes *positive emotions*. For writers, I think this is *so* true. When we are rejected, it is our creative right-brain that generates all of those negative scenes in our mind of an editor tearing out his hair whilst reading our work, saying to himself, "What *makes this writer think they can write?"* We do have a habit of letting our imagination run away with itself!

So this is why, in this book, I have suggested several left-brain strategies that will help you kick-start your logical and reasonable thought processes into generating more positive emotions to overcome these situations. Our left-brain is analytical so use it to examine the evidence and forget about those negative right-brain thoughts. Look at your booster card. Flick through your achievement files. Look at your word count summaries. See the logical evidence that proves your right-brain negative thoughts are sheer fantasies and not facts! Remember, when you start to feel negative, appreciate that this is your right-brain dominating your thinking. Use your left-brain to counteract these thoughts and spur you on to complete your next short-term goal.

It's all too easy to blame other people for rejections. In fact, that is why we do it. It's far easier to blame someone else, than it is to accept the blame ourselves. Use the strategies in this book to keep you focussed on your destination. Keep coming back to remind yourself how to make your journey easier. And remember, there is only ever ONE person stopping you from becoming a positively productive writer...

YOU.

Good luck.
Simon Whaley
www.simonwhaley.co.uk

Index

100 Muddy Paws For Thought 94, 101

100 Ways For A Chicken To Train Its Human 21, 65

100 Ways For A Dog To Train Its Human 1, 2, 64, 69, 138

A Little Bit Of Me Time 63

Achievement Files 56, 58, 182

Australian Writer's Marketplace 139

Best Walks in the Welsh Borders 100

Bestel, Heather 62

Bluffer's Guide to Banking 99

Bluffer's Guide to Hiking 100

Booster Cards 49, 52-5, 56

Brain
Left 89-90, 132, 181-182
Right 88, 90, 98, 181-182

Brain Training 83, 103

Brainwashing 61

Confidence 150

Conscious 73-74, 80

Constructive Criticism 44-46, 134, 148, 174

Correspondence Courses 172-173

Creativity Diary 109-114

Davis, Bette 66

Decisions 73-74

Eavesdropping 102

Endorphins 105

Feedback 43-46, 132, 174

Fillers 129

Fundraising For A Community Project 46, 99

Goals 6-16, 17-24, 113, 160, 178

Griffith, Joe L 16

Habits 47, 54, 80

Hackles, Lynne xii, 36, 99

Hampshire, Vivien xii, 150

Hobbies 100

Holidays 141-149

Ideas 89, 98-104, 170

Inspirational CDs 62-63

Instant Confidence 63

Jefferson, Thomas 66

Just Ten Minutes 63

Letters Pages 57, 125, 128-129

Lists 115-124

Literary festivals 154-156, 166-167, 169

Luck 1, 64-66

McKenna, Paul 63
Moleskine Notebooks 96-97
Motivation 67
Music 61-62

National Association of
    Writers' Groups (NAWG)
    136, 137, 142, 158
National Novel Writing Month
    (NaNoWriMo) 175-178
Networking 132-140, 145, 150
Notebooks 96-98, 179

Parkinson's Law 17
Perry, Diane xii, 21, 64
Personal Opinion Pieces 129
Pets 101-102
Phillips, Julie xii, 76
Photographs 102
Procrastination 120, 122

Recycling 103
Rejection 31-32, 33-40
Relaxation CDs 62
Retreats 144-145
Reviewing
    Goals 17
    Your Work (see Feedback) 41

Rewards 23-26, 169, 179

Self-catering agencies 146
Seminars 141-149
Seneca (Roman Philosopher)
    66
SMART 12-14

Television 73-78
The Power of Calm 63
Time Audit 77-79
Time Standing Order 85
Travel 100-102
Tzu, Lao 6

Visualisation 67-68

Workshops 141-149
Writer's Block 87-92
Writer's Digest 133, 139, 158
Writers' & Artists' 139
Writers' Circles 133
Writing Buddy 26-27
Writing CV 58-60
Writing From Life 99
Writing Magazines 157-158
Writing Organisations 137

**COMPASS
BOOKS**

Compass Books focuses on practical and informative 'how-to'
books for writers. Written by experienced authors who also have
extensive experience of tutoring at the most popular creative
writing workshops, the books offer an insight into the more
specialised niches of the publishing game.